Vocational Business

2

The Competitive Business Environment

Keith Brumfitt, Stephen Barnes, Liz Norris & Jane Jones

Series Editor: Keith Brumfitt

Published in 2001 by:
Nelson Thornes Ltd
Delta Place
27 Bath Road
CHELTENHAM
GL53 7TH
United Kingdom

01 02 03 04 05 / 10 9 8 7 6 5 4 3 2 1

A catalogue record for this book is available from the British Library

ISBN 0 7487 6360 0

Illustrations by Oxford Designers and Illustrators

Page make-up and illustrations by GreenGate Publishing Services, Tonbridge, Kent

Printed and bound in Italy by Stige

Contents

Introduction to Vocational Business series

This textbook is one of a series of six covering the core areas of business studies. Each book focuses on vocational aspects of business, rather than theoretical models allowing the reader to understand how businesses operate. To complement this vocational focus, each book contains a range of case studies illustrating how businesses respond to internal and external changes.

The textbooks are designed to support students taking a range of business courses. While each is free standing, containing the essential knowledge required by the various syllabuses and course requirements, together they provide a comprehensive coverage of the issues facing both large and small businesses in today's competitive environment.

Titles in the series

Book 1   Business at Work
Book 2   The Competitive Business Environment
Book 3   Marketing
Book 4   Human Resources
Book 5   Finance
Book 6   Business Planning

Acknowledgements

The author and publishers are grateful to the following organisations for permission to reproduce material:
Associated Newspapers Ltd, Baby Milk Action, Green & Black's, the Guardian Newspaper Group, the Environmental Transport Association, Kellogg's, the Office for National Statistics, Foxx, Stockbyte and Corel.

Every effort has been made to contact copyright holders, and we apologise if any have been overlooked.

The Competitive Business Environment

Introduction

Competitiveness is the objective of most businesses and economies. In this book you will discover why competitiveness is important to business at the local, national and international level. You will also learn what 'the Market' means and you will find out how and why both companies and the government try to influence the market.

Not all businesses are the same

How competition in the market affects business

What is competition?

One of the main barriers to success is the action of other people. Very few organisations are able to operate without some form of **competition**, whether they are businesses, charities or part of the public sector. Competition is central to the actions of all organisations.

> Competition occurs whenever there are two or more organisations trying to provide the same service or product. Although the amount of competition between organisations varies, it always influences the organisations' actions and their level of success.

CASE STUDY

Mobile telephones

There are now many different telephone companies and it may appear as if all of them are in competition with each other. This may not be the case. The home based telephone providers, compared to the mobile phone industry, are offering a different service to different people with different needs. This means that the home and mobile phone companies may not actually be in competition with each other. It is important for all organisations to recognise who are their competitors to ensure they are able to respond.

ACTIVITY

Who are your competitors?

It seems obvious that mobile phone operators regard themselves as competitors – they are all in the same business and provide the same sort of service. They all appear to have answered one of the important questions for businesses: 'What business are you in?' This sometimes seems obvious but there are often surprises. For example, is the business of British Airways to provide flights or to provide transport? If the answer is to provide flights then they would be in competition with all the other airlines. If the answer is to provide transport, then their competitors might include the Channel Tunnel, the railways and the coach companies as well as other airlines. When customers can switch to other products as well as other suppliers of the same product, the amount of competition is greater than it first appears. If an organisation understands its own business, it can more easily assess who the competitors are.

In the following table, identify who are the competitors for these well known 'businesses'.

Table 2.1

	Competitor 1	Competitor 2	Competitor 3	Competitor 4
Tesco				
Post Office				
Michael Jackson				
Publisher of gardening books				

One of the most useful ways of looking at a business is by finding out the number of competitors in the same industry. Businesses usually face one of three situations: no competitors, a few competitors or many competitors. These three situations create a framework to look at the actions of businesses.

Table 2.2 Who has the power?

	Number of competitors	Do the competitors supply the same product/service?	Example
Monopoly	None	No	Motorway service station
Oligopoly	Few	Yes	Petrol company
Monopolistic competition	Many	No	Shirt manufacturer
Perfect competition	Many	Yes	Video rental shop

(Although there are other suppliers of petrol and food, the motorway service station has a local monopoly as there are no other local suppliers with the same range of products and services.)

The type of competition, as shown by the number of similar businesses, is a good indication of how organisations will behave. If there are no competitors, a monopoly, then a business has more freedom to operate as it wants. When there are a large number of competitors, businesses have to be careful and cautious to ensure they maintain their customers' loyalty.

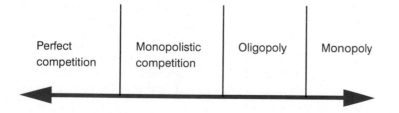

| Perfect competition | Monopolistic competition | Oligopoly | Monopoly |

Figure 2.1 Different market situations

Types of business organisation

The amount of competition is one way of describing organisations. There are other ways to classify organisations and each is useful for particular purposes. Some of the most frequently used systems are:

- the number of competitors
- the size of the business
- who are the owners
- where it is located

- is it in a **primary**, **secondary** or **tertiary** industry
- the type of product or service
- is there a home market, export market or both
- the number of employees.

The economic activity of any country can be divided into three core groups: extractive industries, manufacturing industries and the service sector. These three activities are completed by the primary, secondary and tertiary sectors of an economy. For example, agriculture and mining are extractive industries and part of the primary sector; engineering and assembly work are manufacturing industries and part of the secondary sector; insurance and education are service industries and part of the tertiary sector.

Primary industries

Any business that extracts natural resources is involved in a primary industry. Farming, mining, forestry, oil extraction and fishing are all examples of primary industries. Employment in the primary industries has been declining in the UK as improved technology and more efficient methods of extraction and production reduce the demand for labour.

Secondary industries

A secondary industry is one that transforms the raw materials, produced by primary industries, into products for consumers, for example, manufacturing, food processing and oil refineries. This sector often faces strong overseas competition where developing countries have access to a cheaper labour force. Products such as motorcycles, washing machines and televisions are nearly always imported into the UK, rather than being home produced.

Tertiary industries

Any business that provides a service is involved in the tertiary sector. It includes both business and personal services such as retailing, banking, insurance, computer programming and health provision. This sector has benefited from increased employment prospects as the economy has become wealthier. As consumers' **standard of living** improves, a greater percentage of their income is spent on services.

Key term

The **standard of living** is a way of measuring the wealth of the citizens of any country. The measure takes account of the number of hospitals, the level of social benefits, and the cost of education as well as the income levels of society.

The stakeholder model

Another way of looking at organisations is by the **stakeholder model**. This considers the internal dynamics of an organisation, which are dependent upon a large number of people for its success or failure. Various groups of people are involved with an organisation and they are referred to as the **stakeholders**. Although their interests differ, each group wants the organisation to succeed. It is possible to identify seven main stakeholders for a business:

- shareholders
- employees
- managers
- suppliers
- customers
- community
- creditors.

Each of these seven groups will succeed if the business succeeds and therefore each group has an interest in working together. Although there may be conflicts between the interests of each of the groups, their

collective interests are best served when the business is a success. These
groups can be divided into those who work within the business and
those who are external stakeholders.

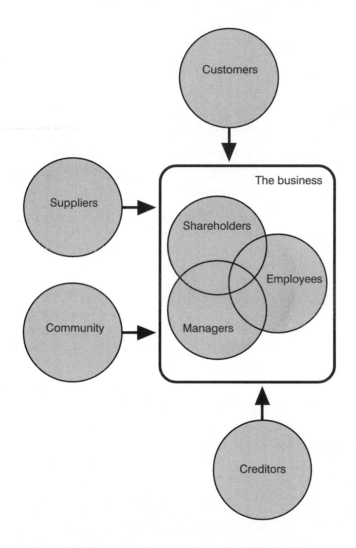

Figure 2.2 Stakeholders

Shareholders

For many decades shareholders were viewed as being the most important
people associated with a business. The shareholders, as owners of the
business, invest their own money and receive dividends if the business is
a success. Shareholders also benefit from an increase in the value of their
shares if the company is successful. These potential rewards of share
ownership compensate for an element of risk. This risk occurs because
share prices can fall and shareholders can lose part of their investment.

Employees

The jobs of those working for a business are dependent on the business's success. This creates a small amount of risk in terms of employment.

Managers

Managers have day-to-day responsibility for running an organisation. Many managers have their salaries and rewards linked to the financial success of the business. This is both a motivation for managers and a means of rewarding their success.

Suppliers

Much business activity takes place between companies as one organisation is the supplier to another. Businesses are often each other's customers and no supplier wants to see a customer facing difficulties.

Community

All businesses operate in their own community, whether this is local, national or international. It is important, not just for the business's reputation, for the business to be respected as an active member of the community in which it operates.

Creditors

Most businesses owe money to other organisations. The people to whom a business owes money are creditors and they are always interested in the business's success. The creditors want to ensure their money is repaid.

Customers

Businesses only survive if they have enough satisfied customers who buy their products or services. Customers are therefore essential to the success of any business and it is important that their views are considered.

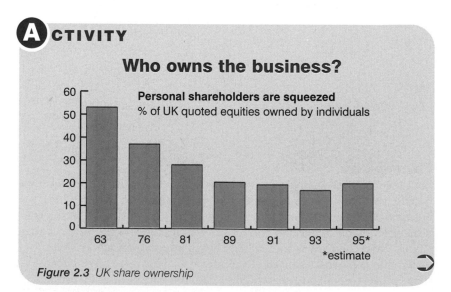

A CTIVITY

Who owns the business?

Personal shareholders are squeezed
% of UK quoted equities owned by individuals

*estimate

Figure 2.3 UK share ownership

Shares in British public limited companies are either owned by financial institutions or individuals in society. Over the past thirty years the number of shares owned by individuals has continued to fall (as shown in the graph) though in recent years this trend has been reversed.

1 Why do you think the number of individual shareholders has risen since 1995?
2 Ask four or five people if they own shares in any British business. Try to discover the following:
   i)   why they own shares
   ii) when they bought the shares
   iii) in which companies they own shares.

What is demand?

There are many things that people wish to own, e.g. a car, telephone, stereo, house, etc. Many of these possessions are needed to survive but sometimes they are wanted to make life more enjoyable. There is a difference between those items that are **needs**, such as water, food, somewhere to live and those items that are **wants**, which are not essential for living, e.g. a television or take-away pizza.

Many people appear to have unlimited wants and always seem to want more and better possessions. These desires are never really satisfied because people keep changing their requirements. If you really want a better stereo, once you have acquired it you might want something even better. Sometimes it not always clear what is a need and what it is someone wants; for example, bread could be essential for survival or it could be something for a party.

Ⓐ CTIVITY

What does he need?

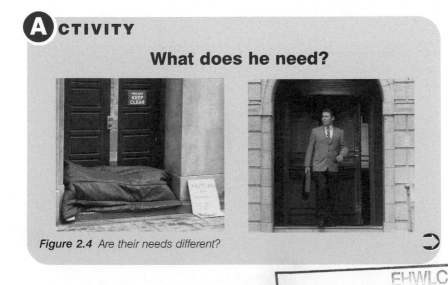

Figure 2.4 Are their needs different?

Consider the two people in the photographs and decide what each of them might need as well as what they might want.

Table 2.3 Wants and needs

	Example	1	2	3	4
The needs of a beggar	Something to eat				
The needs of an office worker	Clothes for the office				
The wants of a beggar	Somewhere to live				
The wants of an office worker	A new car to get to work				

Organisations aim to meet the needs and wants of individuals. If organisations provide products and services that people do not want or need, then they will not be successful. Organisations that provide what people want have met the first requirement of being successful. The second requirement involves providing something that people are willing to pay for. For example, we may all wish to own a very expensive hi-fi system, but no business will be successful unless it can persuade enough people to buy such a product.

The ability and desire of people to pay for something is known as **demand**. Sometimes this is referred to as **effective demand** to reinforce the idea that consumers need the ability to pay in terms of income and spending power as well as the desire to own the product or service. The effective demand for any product will always be smaller than the number of consumers who want to own the product. For example, *Cosmopolitan* may have many more people who wish to read the magazine than are prepared and able to pay for it.

> **Effective demand occurs when consumers have both the ability and the desire to purchase a product at a particular price.**

⊙ASE STUDY

Organic chocolate

A few well known companies supply the UK market for chocolate. These businesses have built up a lot of customer loyalty, since personal preference is very important in determining the demand for bars of chocolate. Green and Black's, established in 1991, was the first company to supply organically grown chocolate to the UK market. The company, trading directly with Central American farmers to ensure they receive a fairer price for their cocoa, has established itself by supplying a different product from that of its competitors. The company has won numerous awards such as the Organic Food

Awards and the Ethical Consumer Awards. In this highly competitive market this new business has survived by knowing that some customers will pay a higher price for their product.

Figure 2.5 *The competition in the market for chocolate*

Ⓐ CTIVITY

The price of chocolate

Green & Black's Maya Gold chocolate currently sells for £1.60 for 100 g. Investigate the price of other similar-sized bars of chocolate in your local shops. Why do you think Green & Black's can charge such a premium price for their product?

In the above example we can identify various factors that influence the demand for bars of chocolate:
- the price of the product
- the price of the competitors' products
- consumer tastes or preferences.

The importance of price in influencing demand can be shown by using a **demand curve**. This shows the amount of Green & Black's Maya Gold chocolate that consumers will demand per month at any price.

> **Note!**
>
> Of all the factors that affect the demand, the most important is the price charged by the business.

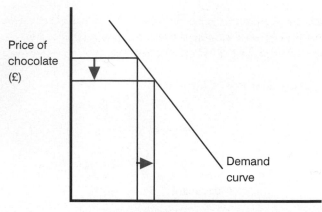

Figure 2.6 *The demand for Green & Black's Maya Gold chocolate*

All businesses know that if they reduce their price, they will be able to sell a larger amount of chocolate to their customers. This is because the product becomes more competitive and more people can afford the chocolate and most consumers prefer to buy more of a product at a lower price.

Ⓐ CTIVITY

Is the price right?

In most years fans have difficulty buying tickets for the final rounds of the FA cup. Fans are often prepared to pay more than the ticket's face value to watch a match. In 1996 it was different. In one of the semi-final matches over 10,000 tickets were left unsold. This was a protest at the high price of between £30 and £38 charged for 86 per cent of the tickets. This high price was more than double the usual price of a ticket for a football league game and the Liverpool and Aston Villa fans were not prepared to pay the higher prices. In the case of Liverpool this was the first time in the club's history that the fans had not bought all the available tickets to an FA cup semi-final match. This is a very clear example of a demand curve where the number of people willing and able to pay falls as the price rises.

1 How important are ticket prices for football fans?
2 What other factors, besides price, will have influenced the demand for these tickets?

What influences demand?

The demand curve is not fixed in one place forever. If any factor that affects demand changes then there will be a new demand curve. Using the case study of chocolate, the following diagram shows the demand for Green & Black's Maya Gold chocolate has risen because one of the

following events has occurred:
- income levels have risen
- the price of other companies' bars of chocolate has risen
- Green & Black's Maya Gold chocolate has become more popular.

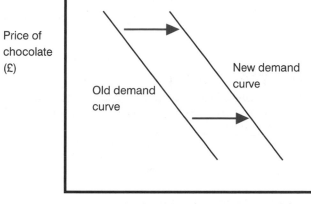

Figure 2.7 *Changing demand for Green & Black's Maya Gold chocolate*

The diagram shows that at each and every price consumers wish to buy more chocolate than in the previous situation before the change occurred. The most important influence on the demand for chocolate as with most products and services is the price charged by the supplier.

The price of similar products

Most businesses operate in a competitive market and need to be aware of their price compared with that of the main competition. Following the privatisation of the railways, there have been three train companies offering tickets from Gatwick airport to London. Each of these companies had a different price for the same journey. Most customers in this situation are very sensitive to price differences and will choose the cheapest train company. If a business's competitors sell a close **substitute**, then demand will be very sensitive to price differences between the similar products.

The price of products bought alongside it

In some industries, consumers are heavily influenced by the price of the accompanying products. The demand for computer hardware or games consoles can be influenced by the price of the software or the games played on the console. If the prices of accompanying products are too high, consumers will switch their spending decisions for both the original and the accompanying products. For example, if one company's mobile telephone charges are too high, consumers will consider another company's phone and associated telephone charges.

Demand for a product is mainly dependent on the price charged for the product. It is also affected by all of the following, which are referred to as the **conditions of demand**:

- the price of similar products (substitutes)
- the price of products bought alongside it (complements)
- the income level of consumers
- the popularity of the product
- how well the product is marketed
- the level of consumer confidence
- the availability of credit
- demographic factors
- seasonal factors.

Elasticity, page 32

Interest rates, page 53

Key terms

Most products and services are classified as **normal goods** because the demand rises for these items as consumers' income rises.
An **inferior good** exists when demand for the item falls as consumers' income rises.

The income level of consumers

For most products or services, demand will rise as consumers receive higher incomes. Businesses selling these items, known as **normal** or **superior goods**, expect demand to rise because:

- existing customers have more money to spend
- there are extra new customers who can now afford the products.

Sometimes demand will fall for some products as income rises. These are **inferior goods** because consumers trade up to better products as they become wealthier.

The popularity of the product

Popular goods have higher demand. If fashion or consumer tastes change then this will affect the demand for products that become popular. This phenomenon is very noticeable with groups and artists releasing records in the UK market. The popularity of each artist obviously affects the demand for records.

How well the product is marketed

Marketing companies and public relations organisations exist to improve the popularity of certain products. Rather than waiting for consumer tastes to change, some businesses try to influence the demand for their goods and services by clever marketing.

The level of consumer confidence

When consumers are confident about the future they are more likely to increase their spending. The increased confidence might be due to:

- more secure employment
- the likelihood of future wage rises
- increase in the value of people's homes.

The availability of credit

Many consumers spend more than they can afford. If it is easy to borrow money or the cost of borrowing is low (interest rates are low) many people will increase their spending. The Monetary Policy Committee of the Bank of England, which is independent of government, meets monthly to set interest rates.

Demographic factors

The age range of the population as well as the size and type of family unit will affect demand. Any country where there is a large percentage of people over the age of 60 (e.g. member states of the European Union) has a large demand for pensions. As the population profile continues to grow older, the demand for savings schemes that provide financial security in old age will rise while the demand for pushchairs will fall.

Seasonal factors

Many products have noticeable variations in demand throughout the year. Greetings card manufacturers expect a large demand at Christmas and on St Valentine's Day. Footwear producers expect demand for sandals to rise in the summer. These seasonal changes can also be influenced by the weather; for example, a warmer than usual summer will increase the demand for sun protection cream.

Want to know more?

If you wondered why consumers want to buy products or make use of services, then you need to consider the benefits they receive. Consumers will wish to buy something if they regard the benefit they receive to be greater than the cost of the purchase. This idea of the consumer's benefit being greater than the cost of the product is called **consumer surplus** and it is what creates consumer demand. If the benefit consumers believe they will receive from a purchase is less than the cost of buying the product, there is no demand. The demand curve shows that at the price (p) some consumers would have been willing to pay more. Their benefit is therefore the difference between the price paid (p) and what they would have been prepared to pay.

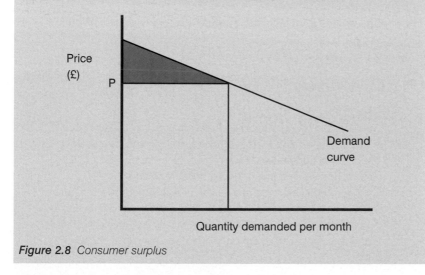

Figure 2.8 *Consumer surplus*

I What is supply?

In order to ensure that businesses meet the needs and wants of consumers, it is important for them to supply the right products and services. If organisations manufacture and sell products and services that consumers wish to buy, then they will be successful. If businesses believe they will receive a high price for their products, they are more willing to

> A market exists when buyers and sellers are able to exchange goods or services at an agreed price. They do not always need to meet or talk as everything could be completed electronically. Markets range in size from local fruit and vegetable stalls to the stock exchange, but they also include every sales transaction from buying a newspaper to selling a secondhand car using the Internet.

trade. As the price of a product rises there are more organisations willing to supply. This happens because the higher prices:

- attract new businesses into the **market**
- encourage existing businesses to increase their output
- encourage existing businesses to switch their production to the more profitable products.

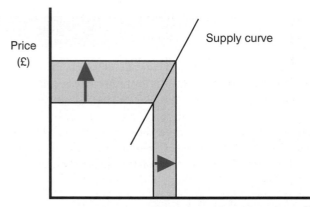

Figure 2.9 *Supply curve*

The supply curve shows that the amount traders wish to sell increases as the price rises.

CASE STUDY

Selling your home

When house prices start to rise, property owners are more likely to put their homes up for sale. At a higher price more people are willing to sell their homes. The higher prices encourage construction companies to build more homes as they are attracted by the higher potential profits. Just because more people are willing to sell houses does not mean they will be sold because this is only one side of the market. The actual number of homes sold also depends on the demand.

> **Note!**
>
> The most important influence on the supply of most products and services is the price the producer will receive for the goods or service.

What influences supply?

In the following figure, at each and every price, the amount people are prepared to supply has risen and a new supply curve is created. This new supply curve has arisen because the conditions of supply have changed. The following factors which influence supply are called **conditions of supply**.

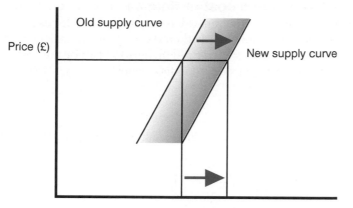

Figure 2.10 Supply curve showing the importance of price

The costs of production

As production becomes more expensive, businesses are not able to supply as much within their budget. In addition, some businesses cannot afford the higher costs and will cease production or go bankrupt as they can no longer make a profit. For both these reasons, as costs rise less will be supplied to the market.

The level of technology

Technological improvements allow businesses to produce a larger amount with the same budget. In addition, new businesses can take advantage of technology and enter the market. For both these reasons improved technology will increase the supply to the market.

The profitability of other products

As any product or service becomes profitable to produce, businesses will switch their production towards the more profitable areas. Profit acts as an incentive for changing output and the supply of highly profitable goods and services rises. The supply of less profitable goods and services falls. If it is unprofitable the supply will cease.

Natural factors, such as the weather

For many products, particularly those dependent on agriculture, natural influences are very important in determining supply. For example, better weather conditions will affect the quantity supplied to the market.

Taxes and subsidies

The government can influence the supply of any product or service by using taxation. If a product is taxed, then the producer is able to supply fewer items with the existing budget. In addition the higher costs, due to the tax, prevent some businesses being profitable. For both these reasons a tax will reduce supply. In a similar way a government subsidy will increase supply.

> **Supply of a product or service is mainly dependent on the price received by the supplier. It is also affected by all of the following:**
>
> - the costs of production
> - the level of technology
> - the profitability of other products
> - natural factors, such as the weather
> - taxes and subsidies
> - the availability and cost of finance
> - economies of scale
> - existence of joint production.

The availability and cost of finance

For most businesses external finance is very important. If businesses are able to borrow easily and cheaply then they are able to expand and increase supply. Whenever credit is difficult to obtain or the cost of loans rises then businesses are forced to reduce supply.

Economies of scale

When an organisation is able to increase its output, there are savings to

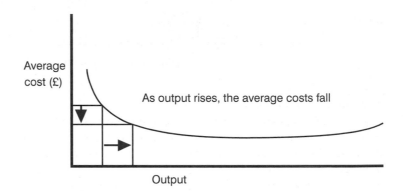

Figure 2.11 Economies of scale

> **Average cost is the cost of each unit. This is measured by the following formula:**
>
> $$\frac{\text{Average}}{\text{cost}} = \frac{\text{Total cost}}{\text{No. produced}}$$

be made. This allows the business to produce its output at a lower **average cost**. This makes production more profitable and hence supply will rise. The existence of economies of scale persuades businesses to increase their supply.

Existence of joint production

When two products are produced together, the increase in supply of one product will lead to an increase in the supply of the other. For example, if the supply of beef rises, then the supply of leather will also rise.

Want to know more?

Businesses compete to make higher profits. Profits and competition are essential parts of a market based economy. There are a few countries in the world where the market economy and competition are not used. These countries have centrally planned economies and the state or government controls most of the economic activity. In such systems, planning organisations and committees make the decisions about what to produce, where it should be produced and what price should be charged. Following the changes in eastern and central Europe very few countries now operate without a system of competition and profit.

I How does a market work?

CASE STUDY

LETSlink

Key terms

A **barter system** occurs when people exchange or swap goods and services without using any form of money; for example, someone swaps two secondhand books for three compact discs.
Equilibrium is a situation when there is no reason to change. When a market is in equilibrium it means the number of buyers equals the number of sellers.

Figure 2.12

Markets exist whenever buyers and sellers agree to exchange something at an agreed price. This does not mean there has to be an exchange of money and in the case of the LETS scheme, a complicated **barter** system has developed. The LETS scheme uses a local 'currency' to allow goods and services to be traded without the need for money. For example, a member of a LETS scheme earns credit by providing childcare, plumbing or cooking for another member in the system. In the UK there are currently over 400 local LETS schemes with 20,000 people creating a market for local goods and services. The LETS scheme creates a market of local buyers and sellers who are able to trade and agree their own prices.

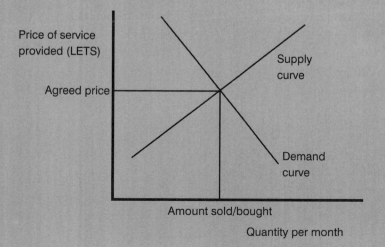

Figure 2.13 Buying and selling using LETS

Within the LETS scheme, buyers and sellers agree how many goods and services they will supply to each other and an **equilibrium** position is reached.

Table 2.4 *Supply and demand schedule*

Price (£)	Supply (thousands)	Demand (thousands)
6.00	400	670
6.20	420	610
6.40	440	560
6.60	470	520
6.80	500	500
7.00	540	480
7.20	580	460
7.40	630	430
7.60	680	400
7.80	750	360

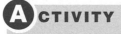CTIVITY

The above demand and supply schedule shows the market situation for a toy. The figures are for the month of July.

1 Draw, with appropriate labels and heading, the demand and supply curves for this toy.
2 At what price does equilibrium occur for this toy?
3 What would happen if the manufacturer set the price at £6.60?
4 What would happen if the price was set at £7.20?

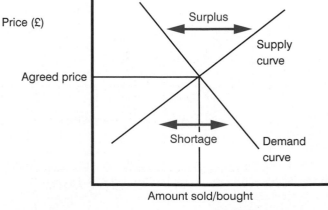

Figure 2.14 Moving to equilibrium

Prices move to equilibrium to ensure there are no surpluses or shortages of products in the market. When prices are too high, suppliers have a surplus as consumers are not prepared to pay the high prices. Suppliers are therefore forced to reduce their prices to sell their products. Many retailers have sales after Christmas, which encourages customers to spend more money besides creating space for new stock.

If the supplier sets prices too low, there is a shortage. Consumers are attracted by the low prices and try to buy more than is available. When this happens two different forces are at work:

1 suppliers realise that prices are too low and increase their prices
2 consumers start to offer higher prices to ensure they are able to buy the things they want.

This second force is particularly important in some markets such as housing, where house prices increase because some purchasers are prepared to offer more than the seller is asking. This also occurs on the stock exchange when share prices rise as purchasers compete to ensure they are able to acquire the shares they want.

Changes to equilibrium

Figure 2.14 shows that equilibrium is a fixed point and the market will not change. All businesses know that a change in the conditions of supply and demand will affect their operations. Supply and demand are not fixed and when one of them changes it will affect the **market price** for products or services.

If the demand rises, for any of the reasons listed earlier, then prices and sales will increase. If the supply rises, for any of the reasons listed earlier or because new businesses start up, then prices will fall as the market becomes more competitive. These two changes can be seen in Figures 2.15 and 2.16.

 Conditions of demand, page 11

Conditions of supply, page 15

Key term

The **market price** or **equilibrium price** is determined when the amount people want to buy equals the amount people want to sell. This is often referred to as the point where supply equals demand.

Note!

Earlier we listed the following factors that could affect the demand curve:
- the price of substitutes
- the price of complements
- the income level of consumers
- the popularity of the product
- how well the product is marketed
- the level of consumer confidence
- the availability of credit
- demographic factors
- seasonal factors.

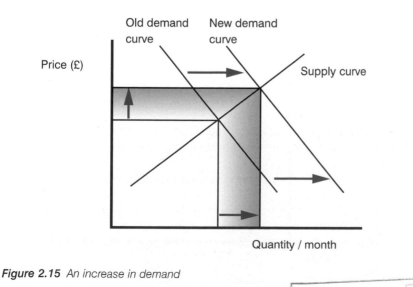

Figure 2.15 An increase in demand

Earlier we listed the following factors that could affect the supply curve:
- the costs of production
- the level of technology
- the profitability of other products
- natural factors
- taxes and subsidies
- the availability and cost of finance
- economies of scale
- existence of joint production.

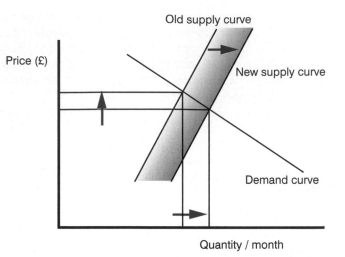

Figure 2.16 *An increase in supply*

ACTIVITY

Using supply and demand curves, explain how the following changes would affect the market for flights from London to Paris:
1   A new airline enters the market
2   The cost of aviation fuel rises
3   The Channel Tunnel closes for four weeks for repairs.

Try to draw a supply and demand curve for each of the three new situations listed above. In each situation show the curves before and after the change to supply or demand. In each of the three cases explain why the market conditions have changed.

ACTIVITY

The following diagram, Figure 2.17, shows changes in the population over 100 years. These changes will affect businesses in the UK as the population becomes older.
1   What is the percentage increase in the number of people over 65 from 1994 to 2031?
2   What is the percentage decrease in the number of people under 16 from 1994 to 2031?
3   Which businesses will benefit from this change in the age distribution of the UK population?

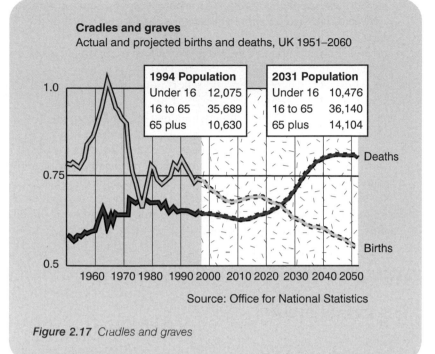

Cradles and graves
Actual and projected births and deaths, UK 1951–2060

1994 Population		2031 Population	
Under 16	12,075	Under 16	10,476
16 to 65	35,689	16 to 65	36,140
65 plus	10,630	65 plus	14,104

Source: Office for National Statistics

Figure 2.17 *Cradles and graves*

Resource allocation

Markets operate as a means of allocating resources. As prices are adjusted, suppliers and customers make different decisions and this ensures that the economy continues to respond to changes. This process of resource allocation can be seen by a theoretical example. For example, if the price of computers rises, companies will be attracted to this business. This means more computers will be produced, more people will be employed in producing computers and more money will be invested in these industries. As all these resources enter the computing industry, they will be taken from other industries which will decline. Resources have moved to the more profitable areas at the expense of less profitable areas.

| What types of market exist?

As we saw earlier, markets exist in all shapes and sizes. Markets are not limited to consumers buying from retailers. Some of the common types of markets are:
- internal markets within businesses, where one section of an organisation sells its output to another section; for example, in a petrol company, the oil refining business may sell its output to the petrol retailing division

- one business supplying another; for example, many construction companies use smaller suppliers as they sub-contract some of the work
- stock exchange markets where representatives trade on behalf of clients
- virtual markets where buyers and sellers never meet, such as those provided by the internet
- employers and employees who create a market for the supply of labour
- public sector markets where businesses complete tenders for the work. This type of market exists when there is no agreed price and businesses submit a price, against the specification in the contract, at which they will complete the work. The contract is then given to the business which offers to complete the work at the lowest price, subject to controls over the quality of the work.

CASE STUDY

A virtual market

More and more businesses have set up home based shopping via the Internet. By the end of 1999 over 13 million people in the UK had access to the Internet and spent over £10 billion. This virtual market allows consumers access to many of the products and services found in the high streets of British cities. Buying clothes, food, records and holidays as well as gaining access to banks, insurance companies and bookshops is now straightforward. This market is open 24 hours a day, the products can be cheaper than in the high street because there are fewer overheads, the market is worldwide and it is quicker to browse through the Internet than visit the various shops. This virtual market has much to recommend it.

CASE STUDY

Virtual holidays

Travel sites are among the most popular sites on the Internet. Many companies, including deckchair.com which set up in 1999, offer a service to customers who wish to book a last-minute flight. Internet based travel companies are very competitive as they do not have to invest in any retail outlets. Many existing travel agents recognise this competition and, in an industry that expects 25 per cent of all holidays to be booked on-line by 2003, are looking at how they will remain competitive.

ⒶCTIVITY

Check out some of these virtual holiday sites to see how their services differ. Look at sites such as www.expedia.co.uk, www.lastminute.com, www.bargainholidays.com, www.city2000.com/travel, www.travelcity.co.uk, www.thomascook.co.uk and www.cheapflights.com

ⒸASE STUDY

The stock exchange

The stock exchange is a market for secondhand shares, where buyers and sellers agree prices. Buyers and sellers are not allowed to trade on the stock exchange – they are required to work through agents, called market makers. These agents act on behalf of their clients.

Key terms

Consumer goods are any items bought by consumers, such as washing machines, radios, etc.
Capital goods are items that increase the productive capacity of businesses such as machine tools, office equipment, buildings, etc.
Personal services are those services such as banking, hairdressers, car repairs, etc, that are provided to consumers.
Business services are those services such as business insurance, accounting services, consultancy, etc, that are provided to the corporate sector.
Industrial goods are manufactured or semi-manufactured products such as washing machines, steel, machine tools and components.
Commodities are naturally occurring raw materials such as rubber, oil, sugar and copper.

The above examples demonstrate markets at work. Whenever buyers and sellers exchange goods or services, they are operating in a market. These markets vary but they all operate in the same way. Markets exist for all sorts of products and services, such as **consumer goods**, **capital goods**, **personal services**, **business services**, **industrial goods**, and **commodities** which are sold in the private and public sectors of the economy.

The variations in the type of market occur because:

■ **the buyer or seller has more power**

■ **the level of competition varies**

■ **the government becomes involved**

■ **it is an overseas market, a home market or both**

■ **it is a product or service**

■ **it is a raw material or finished product.**

Want to know more?

In most industries competition is between existing businesses. In some industries competition is also between potential new organisations and the existing businesses. This is described as a **contestable market** because it is relatively easy for new businesses to set up and therefore existing firms have to continually think about the potential competition. An example of this might be the video rental industry as it is very easy for any existing retailer to start hiring videos.

 e-commerce, page 28

 Marketing strategies, page 24

ⓒASE STUDY

Real and virtual toys

In October 1999, eToys was launched in the UK. The company, having borrowed $1 million to build a website, set out to capture a large share of the toy market. The company's marketing strategy aimed to supply all on-line orders within 3 to 6 days. Compared to traditional toy retailers reliant on retail outlets, costs will be lower. eToys closed in Spring 2001.

I How do businesses increase competitiveness?

To be competitive in an existing, well-established market, new businesses have to offer something different. There are various ways that businesses can do this:

- offer a different product or service
- offer a better quality product or service
- offer the same product at a lower price.

The following three case studies illustrate how different organisations have selected their own strategy to improve their competitiveness. In each situation the organisation is following a successful approach that meets the needs of their market.

ⓒASE STUDY

Breakdown service – a different service

Figure 2.18

There are many companies that offer breakdown services to car drivers. These range from the well known RAC and AA, to the insurance companies and local garages. It is difficult for a new business to compete in this market, but one organisation is managing to. The Environmental Transport Association (ETA) offers something different. In addition to the usual breakdown services, it campaigns for fewer roads, environmentally sound travel policies and alternatives to road transport. This is clearly different from the services provided by the other breakdown organisations and creates a **niche market** for the ETA.

Key term

A **niche market** exists when a group of consumers or buyers have an unusual and specific set of requirements.

In the case of the ETA the organisation is offering an emphasis different from the traditional service and for some people this would be seen as a better service. Obviously not everyone would want a breakdown service that campaigns for fewer cars on the road, but enough people are prepared to pay and this creates sufficient demand for this business.

Ⓒ ASE STUDY

Kellogg's Cereals – better quality

Figure 2.19 *Meeting the needs of customers. (Reproduced by permission of Kellogg's.)*

Businesses will only be successful if they meet the needs of their customers. If these needs can be met at a price that earns a good profit, then all the stakeholders will be pleased. If any organisation can take a relatively low cost input and transform it into a high value brand, there is a very good chance of the business being very successful. The production of breakfast cereals is one area where this can be done. Kellogg's is able to take wheat, rice, corn, sugar, etc, and create well known products that consumers are willing to pay for. As it says on the box, 'Kellogg's Corn Flakes are made in traditional ovens, to a unique recipe which, whilst always striving for higher quality, has produced the nation's favourite cereal for sixty years'. This production process adds considerable value to the raw materials, allowing Kellogg's to earn a profit.

CASE STUDY

EasyJet – a lower price

For passengers wishing to fly to Amsterdam from London, there is a choice of airlines. Most of the carriers fly from either Gatwick or Heathrow, but they are not the cheapest. In 1999, at £38 each way, easyJet charged the lowest price from Luton. This no-frills, ticketless airline cannot compete on access to Gatwick or Heathrow, but it can offer a very good price. This value for money approach is attractive to customers, even if they are not able to fly from the most convenient airport.

The three strategies illustrated in the case studies emphasise the importance of developing a strategy that is clear. This allows all sections of the business to identify with the general approach and ensures that there are no mixed messages. Managers, employees and customers all recognise that each of these three organisations has an effective strategy for competing against other businesses.

Adding value

At the heart of the three strategies is the notion of adding value. This process of adding value to inputs is what enables businesses to be profitable. There are different ways to add value but in all cases the business is providing something the customer is willing to pay for. If the cost of adding value to the inputs, plus the cost of the inputs, is less than the consumer is willing to pay, then the business will be profitable. This ability to effectively add value to inputs and sell the resulting product or service ensures that a business is competitive.

Table 2.5 Added value

Type of business	Raw material	Process of adding value	End product/ service
Petrol supplier	Oil	Oil refining	Petrol
Car repairs	Damaged car	Mechanic's labour	Repaired car
Accountant	Receipts and invoices	Professional expertise	Completed accounts for the tax office
Restaurant	Ingredients	Chef's know-how	Meal
Steel manufacturer	Iron ore and coal	Smelting	Steel

It is the process of changing inputs to outputs which allows businesses to compete effectively. The businesses that are better at adding value are the ones that will be the most profitable.

One way that a business can appear to add value is by advertising. Although the product or service offered may not change, consumers have a higher opinion of the goods and this is sufficient for them to be prepared to pay more. Advertising can be used to:

- promote a brand image
- distinguish the product from the competitors' products
- create a particular lifestyle
- provide factual information.

In all these situations, the consumer is persuaded that the product is of greater value to them and this adds value.

 Consumer surplus, page 13

CASE STUDY

What's the difference?

One of the important roles of advertising is to persuade customers that one company's products are different from those of their competitors. If the advertising is successful then customers are prepared to pay a premium price for their preferred product. Even a **basic** product, such as rice, can be successfully advertised. Uncle Ben's rice is different. It has a brand name. Its packaging is different. All of this is the result of successful advertising. Advertising by itself is not enough, the product must also be of high quality. This will ensure the consumer is satisfied and will continue to purchase the product or service.

Key term

A **basic good** is any product or service that is thought essential for survival.

ACTIVITY

Investigate the prices of other basic products such as wholemeal bread, white bread or milk powder. In each of these cases there are well known products that are heavily advertised. Products such as Hovis, Marvel, and Kingsmill bread are advertised as different from their competitors' products. Are the prices of the well known products always higher than those of their competitors?

Uncle Ben's, like most successful businesses, emphasises the importance of quality in its products. This is an important way of remaining competitive as other businesses can find it hard to produce goods or services to such a high standard. Most of the time, improving quality will increase a business's costs. This may mean the business has to increase its prices.

It is very difficult to be a high quality and a low price supplier, though there are times when improving quality will actually cut costs. By improving the quality control in production, there will be fewer rejects and failures. This allows a greater number of products to be correct the first time. With fewer problems in production, costs can be kept down, thereby allowing low costs and high quality output – a recipe for successful, profitable businesses.

Want to know more?

We can also look at organisations who use e-commerce to become competitive. E-commerce is not an answer to all the problems facing business. There is also no guarantee that having a website will create sales and high levels of profit. E-commerce is one aspect of a business's operations and companies have taken three main approaches. They have:

- set up an e-subsidiary business, separate from the main company
- set up an e-commerce unit within the existing company
- set up e-commerce project teams to handle specific projects.

| How important is price?

For businesses to prosper, as well as survive, they need to remain competitive in their market. As we saw on page 24, there are three main approaches to being competitive:

- offer a different product or service
- offer the same product at a lower price
- offer a better quality product or service.

It is easy to find examples of these approaches to competitiveness in the UK. For example, some of the fast-food outlets provide a low cost product, with good service, and clearly undercut the prices charged by restaurants. These fast-food outlets use all three of the main approaches to improving competitiveness.

A CTIVITY

Investigate the prices of pizza retailers near where you live. There are four main types of business in this market:

- take-away or home delivery
- well known fast-food outlets
- Italian restaurants
- other restaurants.

Complete the following grid to show how these businesses are competing in the same market.

Table 2.6 Take-aways

	Price of pizza	Other features	Is the business competitive?
Take-away or home delivery			
Well known fast-food outlet			
Italian restaurant			
Other restaurant			

Are these four food outlets in the same market? Do they really compete with each other? Using the information from earlier, explain who the competitors are for both the Italian restaurant and the well known fast-food outlet.

Who are your competitors?, page 2

Each time you look at a business you can see the ways in which it is trying to maintain its competitiveness. A business will often use a combination of approaches at the same time. In the following example one business relies on brand loyalty to maintain sales while its competitor relies on lower prices. These battles between businesses, who are all looking for the same customers, happen every day in every market. Businesses have to continually seek to remain competitive.

CASE STUDY

Matching up to the competition

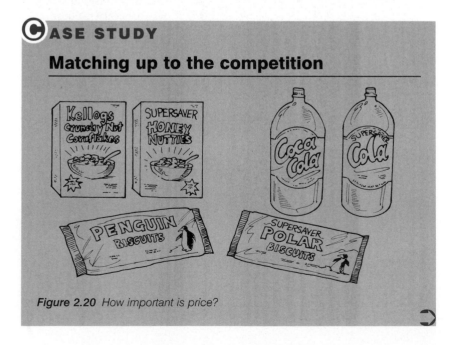

Figure 2.20 How important is price?

Conditions of demand, page 11

 Non-price competition, page 31

Key term

Brand loyalty occurs when consumers buy the same product or service on more than one occasion.

Setting prices is one of the most important tasks for any business since it is one aspect of maintaining or improving competitiveness. Consumers are often very sensitive to price changes and their spending patterns can be heavily influenced by prices. Consumers will switch their allegiance if the price difference between similar products is large enough. Just before Christmas in 1996, one of the UK's largest supermarket chains produced a range of own-brand alcoholic drinks which sold for 75 per cent of the price of some of the leading products. Whether this price difference is enough to encourage a change in spending will depend on the consumer's **brand loyalty** and the marketing effort of the competitors.

Price is clearly an important consideration for customers, but it is not the only factor in deciding which products to buy. The very competitive world of retailing illustrates how different businesses have taken different approaches to remaining competitive and price is not the only area where the battles occur. In the following case studies, each company emphasises non-price aspects of its business as the grounds for competition.

CASE STUDY

Innovation at M & S

Before Marks & Spencer started experiencing financial difficulties in 1999, it had been a very profitable company. It was successful because it provided what the customer wanted. The company's approach, summarised by the statement from the deputy managing director of 'by not owning production ourselves, we sell what the customer wants, not what has been or can be produced', allowed Marks & Spencer to be close to their customers. This meant the business could respond quickly to changes in customers' demands and tastes; for example, a quarter of all the food lines were new every year.

Source: adapted from *The Guardian*, 2 March 1997

CASE STUDY

Encyclopaedia Britannica

In November 1999, Encyclopaedia Britannica planned to change its whole approach to selling and pricing its main product: their plan was that the encyclopaedia would no longer be sold in book or CD-ROM formats – it would be given away. The encyclopaedia would be freely available on the Internet and the owners would make a profit by selling advertising space on the appropriate web pages. This is a modern version of the free local newspapers, which have maintained their competitiveness with the national press.

CASE STUDY

Better service at Tesco

In April 1996, Tesco recruited 4,500 customer assistants whose main job was to help people with their shopping, by packing bags, finding items on shelves and unpacking trolleys. This return to providing a personal service is part of the battle for customers between the main supermarkets.

CASE STUDY

Going cheap

With the takeover of Asda by the American retailing giant Wal-Mart in 1999, supermarkets became more competitive. One of the key approaches to remaining competitive is the 'buy one, get one free' approach. Everyone likes to get something for nothing and these multibuys are a successful way of encouraging consumers to buy products they do not really want.

The case studies have shown various strategies used by businesses to increase their competitiveness. These have included:

- regular new products (Marks & Spencer)
- better quality service (Tesco)
- a free product but a charge for the service (Encyclopaedia Britannica)
- developing brand loyalty (Kellogg's)
- offering a free product and charging for advertising (Encyclopaedia Britannica)
- keeping prices low (easyJet)
- multibuys (Asda)
- distinguishing the product (Uncle Ben's)
- offering a different product or service (ETA).

In addition to these approaches, there are other ways of competing in the market. Examples of these include:

- marketing campaigns
- undercutting the price of competitors
- adapting quickly to changes
- increasing the business's efficiency
- developing a unique selling point.

Want to know more?

Consumers are always changing their spending behaviour. Businesses are interested in finding out why spending behaviour changes and what factors are important. The way of measuring any change is called **elasticity** and it calculates how consumer demand changes as a result of various factors. Consumer demand could change because of:

- the price of the product
- the price of other products
- the level of consumers' income.

Each of these three changes can be measured by elasticity and is recorded as:

- the price elasticity of demand
- the cross elasticity of demand
- the income elasticity of demand.

> **Key term**
>
> **Elasticity** is the way you measure how demand responds to changes in any other influence.

Table 2.7 Elasticity

Explanation	Cause of the change in demand	Type of elasticity
Price falls cause consumers to buy more of a product	The price of the product	Price elasticity of demand
Cheaper substitutes cause consumers to switch their spending	The price of other products	Cross elasticity of demand
Higher levels of income cause consumers to buy more of a product	The level of consumers' income	Income elasticity of demand

> **Key term**
>
> **Diversification** occurs whenever a business becomes involved in unrelated trading activities.

Competing companies

Large businesses also have a greater chance of remaining competitive by selling a range of products or services. This process of **diversification** prevents a business depending on one market for one product or service.

Companies such as Tesco, Asda, Kellogg's and Marks & Spencer all sell a range of products. In some cases these businesses sell completely unrelated products. For example, Marks & Spencer sells a range of financial services as well as food, furniture and clothing. This allows the risks of being in business to be spread across a number of sectors.

 Marketing, page 12

How business is affected by government policy

All UK businesses operate within a market economy. Businesses rely on the smooth operation of supply and demand. If markets do not work efficiently, it is more difficult for businesses to succeed. The market system works when buyers and sellers are able to agree on prices. In a competitive market system there are numerous buyers and sellers, allowing consumers choice between suppliers. Not all markets are competitive and in such situations the market system does not operate as expected. A market is said to fail when supply and demand do not work properly and there are unusual or unpredictable consequences.

> **Markets do not always work efficiently because of:**
>
> - **a lack of information**
> - **merit goods**
> - **externalities**
> - **public goods.**

Why do markets fail?

Lack of information

One of the main reasons for markets failing to allocate resources is a lack of information. We assume that businesses know that they can be profitable if they supply particular products. Businesses cannot be certain of their success; they do not always know there are customers for their products; they do not always know how to persuade customers to buy their products. Consumers often lack information: they do not know whether similar products are available at other retailers or by mail order; they do not always know the prices charged by other suppliers. A lot of things can go wrong when consumers and sellers do not have enough information.

 Resource allocation, page 21

ⒸASE STUDY

The neighbours

Mr and Mrs Sinclair wanted to build a porch outside their home. The builders estimated this would cost £1,800 and the Sinclairs thought this was too expensive. Their neighbour, Ian Kay, was also considering building a porch but could not really afford the expense. Neither of the neighbours were able to proceed until they had met and talked about their ideas. If they employed the builder between them, they would be able to build a cheaper porch that met all their

needs. By sharing information they were able to make a decision
different from the one they would have made if they had acted
independently of each other.

Figure 2.21 *Have you asked the neighbours?*

There are certain goods which are not very well allocated by using
markets. These products and services can be allocated by relying on
supply and demand (the market mechanism) but the results do not
always seem sensible.

Merit goods

CASE STUDY

Public provision?

In the USA there are many private ambulances owned by individual
entrepreneurs. These ambulances collect people who are injured in
accidents and take them to the local hospital. The ambulance owners
are paid by the insurance companies on behalf of those who are
injured. The insurance companies are prepared to pay for privately
owned ambulances because injured people, taken quickly to hospital,
have a greater chance of a fast recovery and this reduces the hospital
charges paid by the insurance companies. This system works
alongside the ambulances that are owned by the hospitals. In the UK
all the ambulances are provided by the National Health Service, often

through local Health Trusts. This is a state organised system where the service of taking people to hospital is provided by the government.

Everyone who pays taxes contributes to the National Health Service, which provides a service everyone can use. If there were to be a market based system some people might not be able to afford health insurance and would therefore be denied the use of privately owned ambulances. The ambulance service is regarded as a 'good thing', something that is beneficial to society as a whole. Such goods or services are called **merit goods.**

Key term

A **merit good** is something that is socially desirable but would not be produced in large quantities without state intervention.

Externalities

Markets can also fail when there are **externalities**. These are the side effects of business activities. They are the costs paid by the wider community. In all economic activity there are private costs and social costs. The private costs, or costs to the business, form the basis for setting prices as they have to be recouped to ensure profitability. The wider social costs include the effects of toxic gases on society, the pollution from delivery lorries or the effects of noise from a company's factory. These social costs, the externalities, are not paid by the business and there is therefore little incentive to take them into account. This means the market is not working properly because the business does not have to consider all the relevant costs in making the decision of how much to supply.

Key term

An **externality** is a benefit or a cost incurred by someone who does not cause the event to happen. For example, a manufacturer who pollutes the countryside causes the residents in that area to have higher costs of cleaning.

Conditions of supply, page 15

Public goods

Governments wish to encourage the consumption of products and services that benefit society as a whole. This is particularly the case when merit or public goods are involved. Merit goods, such as education or health provision, provide considerable benefit to the whole of society. Even when the government encourages consumption of merit goods, it does not mean that the government always has to pay for such goods. For example, governments expect most students in higher education to contribute to their course fees. **Public goods** such as street lighting, libraries, the justice system and the armed forces are provided by the government because everyone benefits from them. If the government did not organise these services, consumers would be reluctant to pay and some people would take the benefits without contributing. For example, many museums do not have an entry charge but ask for contributions to pay for the upkeep of the buildings and exhibits. Some people contribute, others don't.

Key term

A **public good** is something that can be consumed by one person without preventing another person from consuming the same thing.

CASE STUDY

Feeling safe

Figure 2.22 Who should pay for street lighting?

It is obvious that we all benefit from street lighting. It allows us to feel safe at night. It provides light for car drivers and pedestrians. However it is not a free service. The installation, maintenance and running costs have to be paid for by someone. In the UK these costs are paid by the local community in the form of a council tax. Street lighting would not be provided by any market mechanism because no one would be prepared to cover the costs; i.e. people want the benefits of the service but there is no effective demand. This is a public good that is supplied by the state to ensure we can all benefit.

 Effective demand, page 8

Is big business too powerful?

When there is only one supplier, the business is likely to be very successful. This allows such a company to earn high profits. One of the main reasons for a lack of competition in some markets is the power held by large organisations. Sometimes consumers are not able to shop around for the best deal or select between competing suppliers because there is only one company offering goods for sale.

What gives business its power?

The market mechanism assumes that buyers and sellers have equal power and that the market price is determined by agreement between these buyers and sellers. In most situations the sellers have much more power than the buyers. The sellers (producers) offer their product or service at the price they choose and invite customers to buy their goods. If customers are not interested, perhaps because the price is too high, the sellers do not adjust their prices as the market mechanism suggests. The sellers merely try to sell their goods to other customers.

To achieve power over buyers, producers need the ability to control the supply of any product or service. This creates an unequal situation with buyers having less influence.

CASE STUDY

Drugs war

In 1997 Glaxo Wellcome lost its legal protection in the USA for its bestselling medicine, Zantac. This ulcer treatment had a **patent** for 16 years in the USA, which prevented any other company selling the same product. This control over the supply of the medicine had earned Glaxo Wellcome early £20 billion worth of sales. Now the patent has finished, other companies are able to enter the market. This offers consumers more choice and the competition is likely to reduce the price charged for ulcer treatments.

Key term

A **patent** gives its owner the exclusive legal right to use an invention or idea for a prescribed number of years.

▶ Monopoly, page 3

In the above example Glaxo Wellcome had a monopoly over the supply of Zantac and the research that underpinned its development. This monopoly existed throughout the world because patents can be taken out in all countries. This allowed the company to have control over the market for the sale of the product as well as the geographical market. Very few businesses have this level of control over supply. This control exists because there are very few substitutes for the medicine. Control over a geographical market exists because consumers cannot normally go to another part of the country to buy the same product.

ACTIVITY

Consider the following businesses and identify how much power they have.

Table 2.8 How much power?

Example	Control over the market for the product or service	Control over the geographical market
Motorway service station	No power	Very powerful control
Coca Cola		
Local newsagent on a housing estate		
Filofax diary		
The BBC		

Does the buyer have any power?

Markets are often presented as though the buyers are individual consumers and the sellers are large companies. This is not always the case. There are markets where the buyers are the large companies and the sellers are small businesses providing raw materials or a service. On other occasions the buyers and sellers work for the same business and there is an internal market. It is important to recognise that markets exist in all shapes and sizes.

CASE STUDY

Kotecha decorators

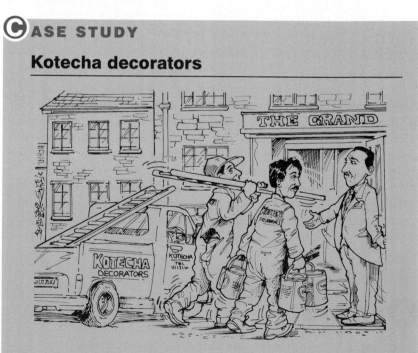

Figure 2.23 An unfair world

Joe Kotecha runs a small family business in Leicester, specialising in upmarket home decoration. At the end of 1999 he won a contract to redecorate a local hotel foyer. This work took three months to complete, but he had to wait another four months before he was paid by the hotel. When the payment arrived, it was 10 per cent less than expected because the hotel claimed that the work was not up to the required standard. Joe was not happy with this, especially since there was only a small profit margin on the work. In December 2000, Joe was offered another contract by the same hotel to redecorate 25 bedrooms. Joe turned down this contract because he felt he would not be able to make any money. His reasons were:

- waiting too long to be paid
- the hotel might reduce the amount they pay
- he will incur a large number of costs before receiving any money
- the contract is too big for a small business.

In some markets the buyer is very powerful and can greatly influence business activity. Where this occurs, **consumer sovereignty** exists and sellers respond to the wishes of their customers. Buyers have most power when there are a great many businesses all competing to sell the same products or services. This allows consumers to 'shop around' for the best buy. This is certainly the case in the above example where the hotel could approach many small businesses to see which decorator offered the best deal.

Is the power of business increasing?

For a business to keep control over its market it has to either continue to control the supply or improve its competitive position. Maintaining or improving a competitive position is time consuming and expensive. Managers have to continually check what competitors are doing and react accordingly. On some occasions the pressure of competition becomes too great and businesses try to work together rather than compete. An obvious effect of this is the reduction in choice for consumers.

CASE STUDY

All at sea

The opening of the Channel Tunnel in 1994 created an additional competitor in the cross-Channel transport market. In 1997 the two largest ferry operators, P & O and Stena Lines merged their operations. This was a response to the increased competition, particularly as a result of the lower prices charged by Eurotunnel. This merger effectively creates a **duopoly** with two large organisations controlling most of the market.

> **Key term**
>
> **Consumer sovereignty** exists when sellers respond to the wishes of their customers. Buyers have more power than sellers in the market.

Who are your competitors, page 2

ACTIVITY

Investigate the cost of travel across the English Channel. Using official brochures and any offers in the newspapers, work out whether the Channel Tunnel or a ferry company offers the best value for each of the following journeys:

- four people with a car who want to stay in France for five nights
- a businessperson wanting a day return to Calais
- four adults with a car and caravan who want to stay in France for two weeks.

How much competition exists between the Channel Tunnel and the various ferry operators? Are airlines the real competitors for the ferry companies and the Channel Tunnel operators?

There are various ways in which businesses work together, without the formal requirement of a merger. Each allows businesses to share information which reduces the level of competition. We saw, on page 3, that there are different types of markets ranging from monopolies to very competitive situations. Each time businesses collude or work collaboratively the amount of competition is reduced and the amount of monopoly power increased.

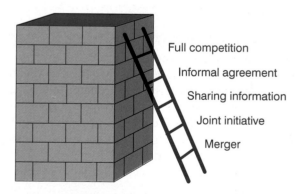

Full competition

Informal agreement

Sharing information

Joint initiative

Merger

Figure 2.24 Reducing competition

- Merger – when two or more businesses join together to create one organisation. A merger can occur when businesses are in a similar market or in completely different markets
- Joint initiative – when businesses work together on a specific project, e.g. Hotpoint washing machines and Ariel washing powder on an advertising campaign
- Sharing information – when one business provides another with information, e.g. a mail order business working with an insurance company on a direct mail campaign

- Informal agreement – when no agreement exists in writing but there is a common understanding between businesses not to compete, e.g. regions of the country are allocated informally to different businesses.

CASE STUDY

Glaxo Wellcome

Earlier we looked at how a pharmaceutical business relied on its patents to control the supply of a highly profitable medicine. Glaxo Wellcome plc was the result of Glaxo successfully bidding, in 1995, to take over the rival business of Wellcome. With a larger product range, the new company was able to compete more strongly in the world pharmaceutical markets.

All businesses try to maintain or increase their control over the market. This gives them power that allows them to be competitive and ensures they continue to make profits for their shareholders. Takeovers and mergers are two obvious ways in which power becomes concentrated in the hands of fewer businesses. Although these activities benefit the shareholders, other stakeholders may not be so successful when takeovers and mergers occur:

Stakeholders, page 4

- customers face a reduction in choice
- some employees and managers may become unemployed as the business is rationalised
- suppliers may find the new business no longer needs their services
- the local community may lose its local employer if there is a reorganisation.

The effects of takeovers, mergers and other anti-competitive actions can be severe and as such the government often has to decide whether they should be allowed.

Want to know more?

Concentration ratios measure the percentage of a market held by the largest three or five businesses in an industry. This gives an indication of the market power of the largest businesses. In the following examples, power is highly concentrated in industry A but not in industry B.

Table 2.9 *Concentration ratios*

% of the market	Industry A	Industry B
Largest firm	12%	4%
3 largest firms	20%	8%
5 largest firms	32%	10%
10 largest firms	50%	12%

Government influence

In 1776 in *The Wealth of Nations*, Adam Smith wrote about the invisible hand that operates in markets. He described a situation where markets worked without outside influence and everything worked for the best. He considered supply and demand as the ideal way for business and customers to work together to meet their mutual wants and needs. Unfortunately, as we have seen, businesses are sometimes very powerful and can have a great deal of influence. Governments become involved in the operation of markets for five main reasons:

- to protect all consumers
- to protect vulnerable sections of society
- to provide goods and services of value
- to restrict production of some goods and services
- to prevent the abuse of power.

Protecting consumers

In any market where buyers and sellers have equal power, there is no need for a government to look after the interests of one side. Unfortunately buyers and sellers rarely have the same amount of power and one side of the market often needs to be protected. In most situations, it is business that has more power and influence than its customers. Businesses can exploit their position of power and take advantage of consumers. Governments are able to protect consumers by introducing a range of provisions such as:

- consumer legislation, such as the Sale of Goods Act and the Trades Description Act
- providing consumer advice
- issuing guidelines to industry and business, particularly on health and safety matters
- setting up watchdogs to oversee industries, such as OFTEL and OFGAS.

Protecting sections of society

Governments protect those in society who may not be able to protect themselves. One main area where protection is needed is the environment. Although it makes good business sense to consider the environment, there are still some businesses that need persuading.

Note!

Pressure groups, by promoting the causes they believe in, can also protect consumers. For example, the Baby Milk Action group on page 71 believes it is protecting consumers in developing countries.

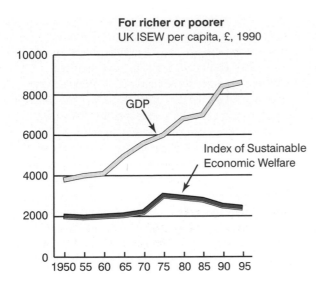

For richer or poorer
UK ISEW per capita, £, 1990

 Economic growth,
page 50

Figure 2.25 *Balancing the books*

As part of the government's approach to protecting the environment, the first Environmental Accounts for the UK were published in May 1998. These identified the amount of pollution caused by various types of economic activity. The graph shows that the country's wealth measured by Gross Domestic Product (GDP) is rising yet when damage to the environment is considered, and if the alternative measure of success, the Index of Social and Economic Welfare (ISEW), is used the UK economy is not so successful.

A second main area of protection embraces groups in society who are not powerful. Many organisations recognise that the benefits of success can be shared between the various stakeholders and so they work within their own industry to prevent exploitation.

ⒸASE STUDY

Living on a shoestring

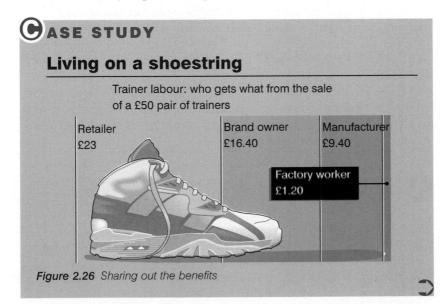

Figure 2.26 *Sharing out the benefits*

Most of the sports shoes sold in Europe are produced in Asia, sometimes in factories with poor working conditions. Christian Aid estimates that only £1.20 from the price of a £50 pair of shoes typically goes to the workers who made the product. Manufacturers are attracted to countries where the cost of labour is low and although there are benefits to the local community in terms of employment, development of skills, etc, there can also be exploitation.

For businesses this is a difficult balancing act. On the one hand companies do not wish to receive bad publicity for exploiting workers in the developing world but on the other hand they are in a very competitive market and need to control their costs. A balance is often found by producers agreeing their own code of practice, which establishes minimum standards and conditions of employment worldwide.

ACTIVITY

In this case, workers are receiving some protection. If the companies had not arranged this, should the government have set controls?

Many businesses face the difficulty of reconciling conflicting economic and social interests. Since all businesses come into contact with various groups in society, as well as other organisations, it is important to recognise that each group will have different needs and expectations. In the above example the sports shoe industry could just ignore the exploitation of Asian workers but this would create bad publicity and possibly affect their sales in Europe. The establishment of an industry-wide code of practice allows all the competing companies, together with the manufacturers, to stop any exploitation. This approach recognises that there are various stakeholders in this industry, all of whom have an interest in its success. European, national and local governments need to be involved to prevent businesses taking advantage of their power and creating problems for society.

Stakeholders, page 4

ACTIVITY

Ageing population

As the average age of society increases, the number of people of working people who have to support the elderly is rising. There is likely to be resentment if those at work have to pay high taxes to support pensioners.

The government can look after both those at work (to limit the amount they have to pay to support pensioners) and those who are retired.
1 What measures could the government take to protect workers from paying too much for the high cost of pensioners?
2 What measures could the government take to protect pensioners from poverty during their retirement?
3 Are there measures to protect both workers and pensioners?

Providing goods and services of value

All governments provide goods and services that are of benefit to society. Both merit goods and public goods can be supplied by local or national governments as services to the community. The government intervenes because private businesses are less likely to supply such products; for example, many local theatres are subsidised by governments.

 Merit goods, page 35

Public goods, page 35

Restricting production

The production and the consumption of some goods and services create harmful side effects. Governments are anxious to avoid these side effects, called externalities, because people who are not involved in the production suffer the costs. An obvious example of a product which has side effects is cigarettes. The health service has to cover the costs of ill health caused by tobacco. In America there have been a number of legal cases by state health authorities against the tobacco companies. In these cases the authorities have received compensation to cover the costs of looking after people whose health has been damaged by cigarettes.

Externalities, page 35

Note!

The structure of an industry is a way of looking at how many competitors operate in the same market.

Preventing abuse of power

A basic belief of free market economies is that competition is beneficial to consumers and society at large. Governments try to encourage competition to give consumers more choice and lower prices. When the market is working effectively businesses compete against each other and the interests of consumers are protected. Sometimes markets do not work in the best interests of consumers and on such occasions the government can decide to intervene.

Competition policy is an important way of protecting the interests of consumers and businesses. The focus of the government's intervention is two-fold:
* to consider the structure of a particular industry
* to react to the behaviour of particular firms in an industry.

British policy on competition is controlled by the Monopolies and Mergers Commission (MMC), though British businesses which operate in a European market are also controlled by European Union legislation. The focus of this legislation is whether the structure and behaviour of businesses is in the 'public interest'.

The UK government's view on competition and its importance is very clear: 'Competition is an essential element in the efficient working of markets. It encourages enterprise, productivity and choice. In doing so it enables consumers to buy the goods they want at the best possible price. By encouraging efficiency in industry, competition in the domestic market also

 Concentration ratios, page 41

contributes to our international
competitiveness. The overall
aim of United Kingdom
competition policy is to
encourage and enhance the
competitive process. When the
process is adversely affected,
the law provides a number of
ways in which the situation can
be examined and, if necessary,
altered. Competition is not
regarded as an end in itself.
With some exceptions, there is
no assumption that a particular
type of action or a particular
situation which reduces
competition is wrong in itself.
The legislation provides for
case by case examination and
only when a matter is found to
be, or likely to be, against the
public interest can it be
prohibited.'

Source: Office of Fair Trading,
1990

The European Union's view on
competition is very clear and
was set out in 1984:
'Competition policy has as its
central economic goal the
preservation and promotion of
the competitive process, a
process which encourages
efficiency in the production and
allocation of goods and
services, and over time,
through its effects on
innovation and adjustment to
technological change, a
dynamic process of sustained
economic growth. In conditions
of effective competition, rivals
have equal opportunity to
compete for business on the
basis and quality of their
outputs, and resource
deployment follows market
success in meeting consumers'
demand at the lowest possible
cost.'

CASE STUDY

Where is the competition?

In 1997, after two years of investigation by the Monopolies and
Mergers Commission, the government announced that manufacturers'
practice of using recommended retail prices for some electrical goods
will be stopped. Before this announcement every retailer used the
same recommended retail price, though some discounts were offered.
This reduced the level of competition between retailers and was
thought to be against the public interest. The government view was
that 'The Monopolies and Mergers Commission has found that
competition in these markets is muted, new retailers have difficulty
getting supplies, and innovation in retailing is discouraged.'

ACTIVITY

Identify one electrical product that you could buy from a number of shops
near where you live. This could be a hi-fi, a washing machine, a freezer or a
walkman. Find out the following information from four different suppliers,
including one that sells through the Internet:
• the price
• what discounts are available
• the price after the discount.
Compare your results with those of other people in your group and decide
how competitive these suppliers are over a range of electrical products. If
price competition is not important, how do you think these businesses
compete?

The UK government, through the Monopolies and Mergers Commission,
tries to discourage anti-competitive behaviour in the UK. European
Union legislation protects consumers whenever a business operates in
more than one European country. The Treaty of Rome, which formed
the legal basis for the establishment of the original European Union, set
out two main aspects of competition legislation:
• Article 85. This prevents any restriction to competition through the
creation of mergers or monopolisation of a market. This part of the
treaty aims to deter any anti-competitive action between two or
more organisations.
• Article 86. This prevents the abuse of a dominant position within
any market. This covers actions by one organisation and there is no
need to show that another organisation is involved. The concept of
market dominance is defined according to the share of the market
or the size of the company or any other relevant factor such as the
range of products.

Government control of the economy

All economies experience periods of growth and decline. This is part of the natural economic cycle. As the economy grows, businesses are able to expand and prosper and this creates wealth for all the stakeholders. When the economy declines some businesses are forced into bankruptcy, while others find that their profits are reduced.

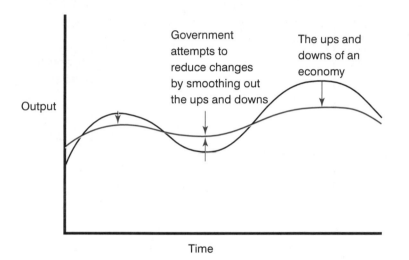

Figure 2.27 Economic cycle

It is possible to identify four stages of the economic cycle:
- expansion, when the economy is growing
- boom, when the economy is at its peak
- recession, when the economy is in decline
- depression, when the economy is at its lowest point.

The government tries to minimise the extent of the economic cycle as a means of protecting businesses and citizens. In a period of economic decline, overall demand will fall and this creates problems for some businesses. This also creates problems for the government because each time a business collapses there are costs to be paid:
- people become unemployed and the government has to pay benefits
- the government receives less income as the unemployed do not pay income tax
- corporation tax receipts will fall
- the UK has to import more if it is unable to produce goods and services itself
- there are social costs, e.g. increases in depression and divorce, as unemployment rises.

 Demand, page 8

The national economy

The economy is made up of a large number of individual markets for goods and services. These markets all have their individual supply and demand curves. These individual markets can be added together to represent the whole of a country's economy. This is shown by using aggregate curves, which indicate the total supply and total demand at any one moment in time. These curves show the price level in the economy and the level of national output. The vertical axis shows the price level, changes in which can be used to measure inflation. The horizontal axis shows national output, which is related to employment levels. The horizontal axis can also be used to indicate the level of unemployment.

Key terms

Aggregate demand is the total spending in an economy. It is made up of all the spending (both in the UK and overseas) by consumers, industry and the government.
Aggregate supply is the total production in the economy. It is the collective output of each producer in the public and private sector.

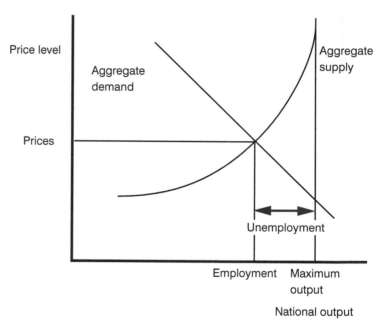

Figure 2.28 Aggregate demand and supply

Figure 2.28 is a simple way of representing the national economy. It can be used to look at changes that affect the whole of society, rather than the supply and demand for one business or service.

ACTIVITY

Aggregate supply and demand diagrams show the national economy as though all the different sectors could be combined easily. In the following chart there appear to be two parts to the British economy – manufacturing industries and the service sector. From 1997 to 2000, the economy entered a period of fast economic growth, a boom, and the service sector continued to expand faster than manufacturing. There were two reasons for the differences between the two sectors of the economy:

- The high value of the pound made it difficult for businesses to export their goods and services. The manufacturing sector is affected because it depends on overseas sales.
- When the economy expands, manufacturing industry cannot increase its output quickly because it has to invest in expensive machinery and it takes time to raise the necessary finance and install equipment. Manufacturers also need to be sure that the expansion in the economy is permanent, as their investment has to be long term. It is easier and quicker for the service sector to increase its output as there is less need for expensive capital investment.

1 What strategies could a manufacturing business use to take advantage of an upsurge in demand caused by the growth of the economy?
2 Why would the government be concerned that the two sectors of the economy were developing at a different pace?

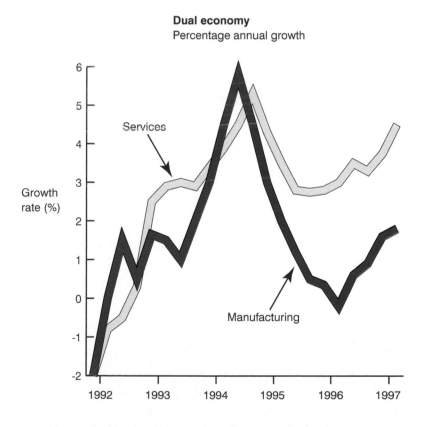

Dual economy
Percentage annual growth

Figure 2.29 The dual economy

What can the government do?

All governments intervene in the operation of market forces (the interaction of supply and demand). This is done to try to improve the success of the economy. The amount of intervention or influence varies depending on which political party is running the government. The whole economy can be influenced (a macro policy) or an individual industry or firm (a micro policy) can be targeted. These macro and micro policies allow the government to influence the actions of individual businesses as well as consumers in society.

Promote economic objectives

In trying to influence the economy, the government has four key economic targets:

- the rate of economic growth – this is a measure of how fast the economy is growing
- the rate of inflation – this is a measure of how fast prices are rising
- the level of unemployment – this records the number of people available for work who do not have jobs
- the balance of payments – this measures the amount of money coming in and going out of the country in one year.

Economic growth

Whenever the productive capacity of the economy increases, there has been economic growth. It is measured as a percentage change from the previous year and is used as a way of estimating the success of an economy. If the economy grows by 2–3 per cent per year this is a good sign. If the economy grows faster than this, there is a risk of inflation.

Inflation

Inflation occurs when prices rise. This is caused for two main reasons: costs of production rise or the demand for goods and services rises. In both cases producers respond to the pressures and put up their prices. The government aims to keep inflation at 2.5 per cent per annum.

Aggregate demand, page 48

Unemployment

This is defined as those who wish to work at the going wage but are unable to find a job. There are two main reasons for unemployment: structural change in society and a lack of demand. Changes in the structure of industry, such as the use of gas rather than coal in the production of electricity, result in a changing pattern of employment and people are made unemployed. This has happened throughout UK history with the decline in the UK textile industry, the UK shipbuilding industry, the UK motorcycle industry, etc. The other main reason for unemployment, a lack of aggregate demand, occurs during a recession or slump. This causes problems for people throughout the economy as all sectors are affected.

Balance of payments

This is a record of the UK's financial position with other countries. It enables the government to find out whether more money enters the country than leaves it. Money enters the country when foreign firms invest in the UK or UK based businesses sell goods abroad. Money leaves the country when British consumers buy foreign goods or British based businesses invest overseas. The government aims to ensure that there is a surplus on the yearly balance of payments. These four economic targets, or objectives, provide a good indication of how successful the government has been in regulating the economy.

The economic climate created by the government is of considerable importance to businesses as it provides the framework for long-term planning. All businesses prefer stability and it is the role of the government to provide the necessary economic stability for businesses to succeed.

ACTIVITY

Complete the following table to show how success with economic policy would benefit businesses in the UK.

Table 2.10 *Economic objectives*

Economic objective	Impact on business
High economic growth	
Low rate of inflation	
Low level of unemployment	
Surplus on the balance of payments	

Changing aggregate demand and supply

Whenever the government introduces large-scale (macro) economic changes, the total supply or demand in the economy will change. Large-scale policies have an impact on most, if not all, members of society. They are designed to have an impact on the economic cycle, as shown in Figure 2.27 on page 47, and reduce the ups and downs in the national economy. The following policies would have such an impact, and can be shown by using aggregate demand and supply curves.

Table 2.11 *Aggregate demand and supply*

Increase aggregate demand	Increase aggregate supply
Reduction in taxation	Increase incentives to businesses and individuals
Increase government spending	Cut down on 'red tape'
Reduce interest rates	Tax incentives on investment
Lower the value of the exchange rate	Reduce interest rates

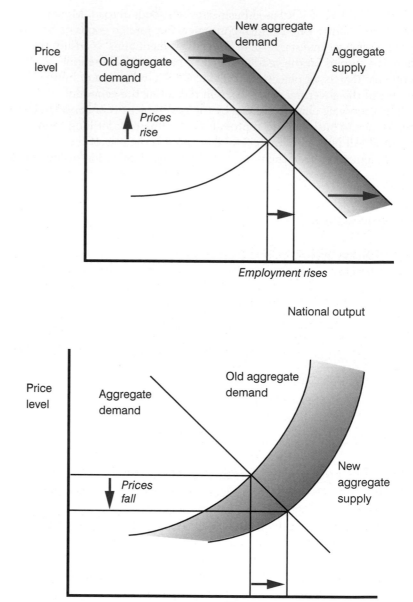

Figure 2.30 *Changing aggregate
demand*

Figure 2.31 *Changing aggregate
supply*

Exchange rates

Whenever there is trade with other countries, the relevant exchange
rate is used. Any change in the value of the exchange rate affects the
cost of buying and selling overseas. When the value of sterling (£) rises,
our currency is more expensive and other currencies are cheaper. This
makes any overseas product cheaper. It also makes British goods more
expensive for overseas buyers. The effect of this is to:

- increase the volume of imports into the UK
- reduce the volume of UK exports.

In a similar way if the value of sterling (£) falls then British goods are cheaper and exports rise while imports fall. The government has limited control over the value of sterling as its day-to-day value is determined by market forces. If international investors have confidence in the UK's economy they will invest in the UK. This causes a rise in the demand for sterling and the exchange rate rises. If international investors lose confidence in the UK's economy the exchange rate will fall.

With the introduction, in 1999, of the Euro currency in eleven European countries many people in the UK began using two currencies. The Euro, a virtual currency until 2002, is used widely by people throughout continental Europe, with the result that many retailers and suppliers price their goods in two currencies.

 Exchange rates, page 66

 Market forces, page 23

The role of interest rates

Until June 1997 the government controlled interest rates in the UK. This power is now held by the Bank of England, thereby ensuring that there is an independent view on the best rate of interest for the UK economy. Each month the Monetary Policy Committee of the Bank of England decides whether to increase or decrease interest rates in the UK. The following table highlights the effects of a change in UK interest rates.

Table 2.12 Interest rates

Increase interest rates	Decrease interest rates
The cost of borrowing rises and consumers have less money to spend	The cost of borrowing falls and consumers spend more money
Businesses face higher lending costs and are forced to put up prices	Businesses' costs fall and higher profits are earned
Businesses put off their investment decisions because of the cost of loans	Businesses bring forward their investment decisions
As mortgages and prices rise, employees ask for higher wage rises	Consumers feel wealthier and there is reduced pressure on wage levels
Overseas investors, attracted by higher returns, put money into the UK. This causes the value of the £ to rise	UK investors go overseas for a better return and the value of the £ falls

In addition to using these macro economic policies, the government can influence the actions of individual industries and businesses with smaller-scale (micro) policies. There are a large number of such policies that could be used.

CASE STUDY

Supporting organic farmers

The demand for organic food is growing rapidly but the British food industry is currently unable to meet this demand. Much of the organic food sold in supermarkets has to be imported. In the UK only 0.3 per cent of farmland is used for organic farming. In other European countries the figures are much higher; for example, in Germany it is 10 per cent, Austria 10 per cent and there are plans for 50 per cent in Denmark. To encourage organic farming the UK government intends to increase the subsidy to farmers who wish to convert to organic farming. The economic benefits of this would be large:

- the level of imports would fall as the UK could produce more of its own organic food
- organic farming is more labour intensive and therefore rural employment would rise
- the balance of payments would improve.

There may also be some environmental benefits as farmers use fewer pesticides.

> **Note!**
>
> Figure 2.32 shows ordinary supply and demand curves, and not aggregate curves, because the subsidy affects only one industry.

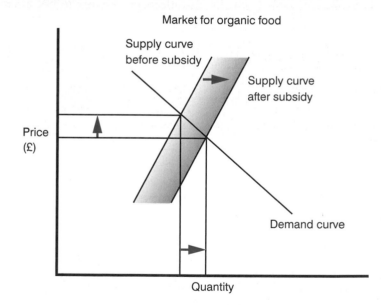

Figure 2.32 Applying a subsidy

Subsidies

The government can encourage production or supply by giving a grant or providing a subsidy for each product. A grant or a subsidy allows existing producers to increase their output or allows new businesses to start up. As the supply rises, the price of the subsidised product falls. This is good for consumers as they can afford to buy more of the cheaper product.

The cost of subsidising products (or businesses) is paid from money raised from taxpayers. It is not something that is free. The government cannot subsidise every type of business because it has limited funds and has to work within its own budget constraints.

Corporate taxation

The opposite effect of providing a subsidy to encourage businesses is to apply taxation. A tax on companies, or the products and services they produce, restricts businesses. The taxation has to be paid from the business's budget, leaving less money for production. Businesses can respond by putting up their prices, if consumers are willing to pay the higher prices. If consumers are not willing to pay a higher price, the business will earn lower profits or have to reduce its level of production.

Taxes act as a disincentive for new businesses to set up. A tax on certain businesses is a micro policy since it only affects some companies. A tax on individuals, such as income tax, is a macro economy policy since it affects everyone who earns money.

Government impose taxes on businesses and their products for two main reasons:

- as a way of raising government funds, such as the tax on insurance
- to discourage production of harmful products, e.g. by putting a tax on tobacco.

 Externalities, page 35

Externalities, page 35

Want to know more?

Businesses whose products have an inelastic demand curve are able to increase prices in response to an increase in taxes. Those whose products have elastic demand curves are not able to increase prices.

Elasticity, page 32

Other policies

In addition to these micro policies there are other ways for the government to influence the economy. Some of these are as follows.

Privatisation

The Conservative governments of 1979–1997 introduced the policy of selling nationalised industries to individuals and private companies. The proceeds from these sales went to help finance other government spending priorities. The newly formed privatised companies are free to operate in the market economy and compete with other businesses. Many of the former nationalised industries have been very successful in earning high profits for their shareholders.

Changing welfare support

Many people in the UK, such as pensioners, students, people with disabilities, etc, receive benefits from the government. These benefits can be changed to reflect government's changing priorities. When the amount of benefit paid is reduced, or increased, the recipients change their behaviour. For example, if the government cut the amount of pension given to retired people, more elderly people would have to look for part-time work.

Buy British

Encouraging consumers to buy British products and services is one way of helping British business. During a dispute, in 1999, over the quality of British and French food some British newspapers encouraged their readers to buy British. For French food producers, with sales to the UK of £2.7 billion per annum this had a significant impact on exports.

Figure 2.33 *Encouragement from the* Daily Mail *to buy British (Reproduced by permission of Associated Newsapers Ltd)*

ACTIVITY

Would it be right for the government to encourage British consumers to boycott French products?

I How the drive for international competitiveness affects business

Encouraging free trade

In economic terms, competition brings about more efficient production, lower costs and lower prices. Competition also encourages **innovation** and allows consumers greater choice. Most national governments, and the European Union (EU), try to encourage competition between businesses because of the advantages to consumers. In an increasingly competitive world market, many British businesses are just as likely to be in competition with European or American companies as with other British firms. **Free trade** aims to create a 'level playing field' where all businesses have an equal chance to sell in any world market.

Helping world trade

Since 1947, the General Agreement on Tariffs and Trade (GATT) has attempted to remove barriers to trade. Its aim has been to introduce wide-ranging agreements to reduce trade restrictions between countries. In April 1994, the last agreement for GATT was completed and this led to:

- further reductions in world trade barriers
- the establishment of the World Trade Organisation (WTO) whose task is to monitor how well countries meet the GATT agreements
- the start of the General Agreement on Trade in Services (GATS).

Most economies operate a free trade policy though there are often hidden ways of protecting home industries. The WTO provides a forum for trade disputes and attempts to ensure that any hidden support or subsidies are removed. The WTO does not have the power to enforce the removal of protectionist policies and has to operate within a framework of encouraging, persuading and entreating countries to endorse free trade policies.

Barriers to trade, page 59

The European Union

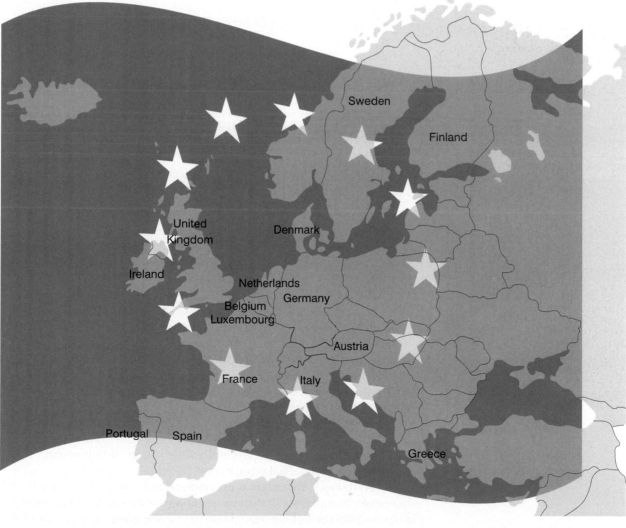

Figure 2.34 *Expanding the market for business*

One of the reasons the UK joined the European Union in 1973 (though it was then called the European Economic Community) was to gain access to a larger market for British business. The EU operates as a 'customs union' where all the member states can trade with each other without any restrictions or tariffs. There are only tariffs or taxes on products that are sold in the EU and produced outside the customs union. The Single European Act came into force in the UK on 1 January 1993 and created a single trading area within Europe. The consequences of this legislation were far reaching for British business. Some of the main effects were as follows:

 Economies of scale, page 16

- the introduction of common EU-wide standards
- the increased possibility of economies of scale because of the size of the EU market
- no restrictions on the internal movement of labour or capital within the EU
- if a product can be sold in one EU country, then it can be sold in all EU countries
- any subsidy given by a government to an industry can be investigated by the EU to see if it gives an unfair advantage to one country's industry.

CASE STUDY

What's in a name?

The Euro, established on 1 January 1999, fixed the currencies of eleven European countries. Each member of this European Monetary Union (EMU) will continue to use its own national currency for three years, during which time the Euro will be a virtual currency. Although the exchange rates of the eleven member states are fixed against each other, the Euro will 'float' against the US dollar, sterling and other world currencies.

Doing business within the European Union

Any business that believes it can operate without the threat of international competition is living in the past. The decline in the number of fish and chip shops from 40,000 to the current 9,000 outlets shows the impact of foreign competition. This has been caused by the increase in American-style burger bars, Chinese take-aways, Indian restaurants, Italian pizza outlets and a wide variety of Indonesian, Korean, French and Thai restaurants.

International competition is everywhere and it is important for British businesses to recognise that there are opportunities to sell overseas. The European Union is the most obvious overseas market for most British businesses. It is easily accessible and there are very few trading restrictions. The 400 million people in the EU create many diverse markets where consumers have different tastes and preferences. This allows British businesses to find a market for their products somewhere in Europe. For example, some British-made goats cheese may be very popular in northern Portugal but disliked in France.

For those businesses wishing to sell in Europe, one of the first decisions is whether to adapt the product or service for this market. Many British retailers have decided not to adapt and it is possible to buy wine from Sainsbury's French branches, or cosmetics from the Body Shop in many European countries. Many smaller businesses, without well known reputations and brand loyalty, will need to adapt to the local market conditions. This will involve making changes to the business's existing arrangements, such as:

- setting up an overseas distribution network
- using local agents in the overseas market
- invoicing according to another country's system
- working with a foreign currency.

Because so many people in the UK have travelled to continental Europe, usually on holiday, there is no longer a fear of working and trading in these markets. As the Euro becomes accepted as the major European currency, any of the doubts business had about European trade are likely to be finally removed.

ⒸASE STUDY

How much is that?

In many hypermarkets in France, the introduction of the Euro currency saw the creation of a third set of prices. Produce that is already priced in francs and sterling is now shown in Euros. Consumers can select which currency they wish to use, though any change is given in francs.

Are there barriers to trade?

There are some occasions when governments try to protect their home industry from overseas competition. Some of the reasons for providing protection from external producers are:

- it allows home based industry to develop
- employment is protected and this prevents the government having to make social security payments
- industries involved in national security have to be supported
- supporting high profile and important industries is a popular measure with the local population.

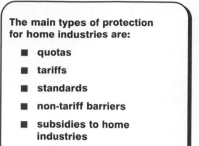

The main types of protection for home industries are:

■ quotas
■ tariffs
■ standards
■ non-tariff barriers
■ subsidies to home industries
■ voluntary restraints
■ foreign exchange controls.

Want to know more?

Quotas and tariffs

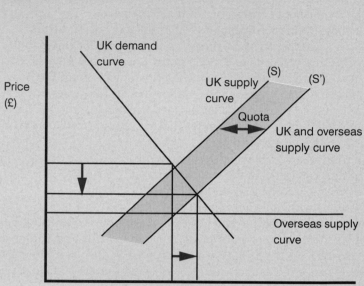

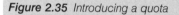

Figure 2.35 Introducing a quota

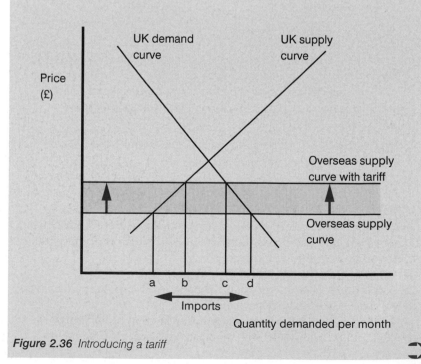

Figure 2.36 Introducing a tariff

A quota places a limit on the number of goods that can be imported. This protects the home based industries but causes consumers to pay a higher price than they would if they could buy everything from overseas. In Figure 2.35, consumers are prevented from access to the overseas supply curve where products are offered at a lower price. The quota allows some of the world producers into the home market and this has the effect of increasing the available supply, from S to S'. The rise in supply reduces the price to the home consumers compared with only having access to the home produced product. The consequence of protecting home industries from the competition of lower prices on the world market is that home consumers have to pay a higher price than overseas consumers who have access to goods at the world market price.

A tariff is a tax on an imported product. It has the effect of increasing the price of imported goods and making the home based product relatively cheap. This supports the home based industry, and provides revenue for the government but results in higher prices for consumers. In Figure 2.36, without the tariff consumers will purchase (d) of the product. Of this amount (a) will be home produced and (d–a) will be imported. With the tariff consumers purchase a lower amount (c) of which (b) is home produced and (c b) is imported. The effects of the tariffs have been:

- consumers pay a higher price
- home producers increase their sales
- the government collects extra revenue from the tariffs.

Trading blocs

CASE STUDY

NAFTA

Many areas of the world have tried to get the benefits of competition as well as the benefits of protection. This is achieved by forming a trading bloc where a group of countries agree to have free trade within the group but to protect themselves from any country outside the group. Well known examples of this type of agreement, called a customs union, include:

- the North America Free Trade Area of the USA, Mexico and Canada (NAFTA)
- the Asia-Pacific Economic Co-operation forum (APEC)
- the European Economic Area, which includes the EU and three other European countries (EEA).

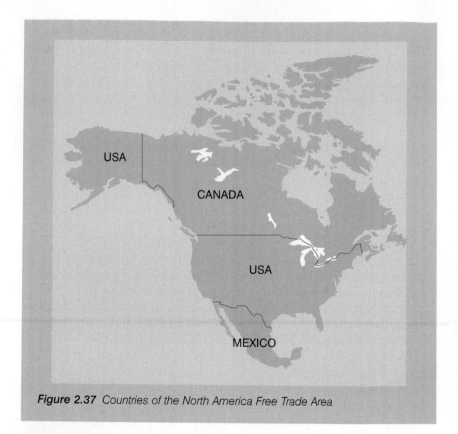

Figure 2.37 Countries of the North America Free Trade Area

Trading blocs allow member states to trade as though they are part of the same country. There are still different currencies within each country but there are no taxes on trade. The European Union began in 1957 as a customs union but has since widened its role to include the removal of all barriers to trade. The introduction of the Euro currency in some countries of the EU is a further removal of trade barriers as the inconvenience and costs of changing money have disappeared.

Non-tariff barriers

CASE STUDY

Electric plugs

Going on holiday in Europe will cause you to think about electricity. Will you need an adapter for any electrical appliance? Will there be enough power to use a hairdryer in the hotel? For anyone who has experienced this problem, it is clear that there are different electrical systems in the European Union. This creates a barrier to trade for business since there isn't one standard system. No country is

attempting to prevent competition but it creates problems for British
companies wishing to sell electrical goods in Italy, Germany or Spain.
This is a non-tariff barrier as the standards adopted in one country are
not the same as in another.

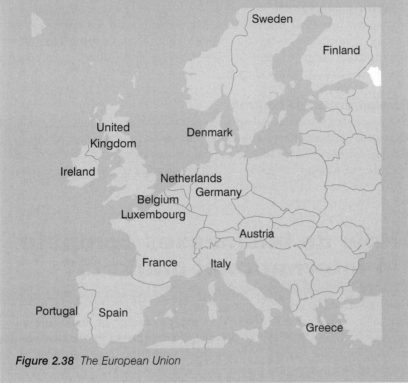

Figure 2.38 *The European Union*

Other types of non-tariff barriers include:
- different labelling requirements; for example, all the writing on a
  product's packaging has to be in the language of the importing
  country
- cultural differences towards imported goods; for example, selling to
  Japan is notoriously difficult
- pressure groups in one country can persuade consumers not to buy
  the produce of another country; for example, many UK consumers
  boycotted South African products in the 1980s
- strict regulations on pollution.

 Tariffs, page 61

Quotas, page 61

Other trading barriers
Subsidies
There are many ways in which governments can protect their home
based industries. Many of the measures, such as tariffs and quotas, are
highly visible to overseas producers. Other schemes such as a subsidy to
the home producer can more easily be hidden. The subsidy allows home
producers to reduce their prices so that they can compete more easily.

Standards

As with the case of electric products, setting a standard for overseas producers to meet could prevent some competition. A standard is sometimes set to maintain safety standards.

Voluntary restraints

Companies can enter into voluntary agreements with the governments of some countries, whereby they agree to limit their exports. This allows the company access to some overseas markets while allowing the country time to develop its own industry.

Foreign exchange controls

Some countries, such as Albania, do not allow their currency to trade on the world markets. As a result these citizens have limited access to foreign currency. This makes it difficult for an overseas producer to sell because the foreign currencies which are needed to pay for the products or services are in limited supply.

▌How do businesses compete in international markets?

Selling overseas is not the same as selling in the home market. Businesses may decide to adopt a pricing, production or marketing strategy in their export market that is different from the one they would use in their home market. In every export situation, businesses can expect to face competition from other exporters as well as from the local producers. Large, multinational businesses who have well known brand names can rely on their reputation in the home market to sell overseas. Small and medium sized businesses will have to create their own reputation in each export market. The following three case studies illustrate some of initial problems businesses face when selling overseas.

▶ Brand loyalty, page 30

ⒸASE STUDY

Do you know the market?

For Cadbury's or any other UK chocolate producer selling overseas, there is a need to know a great deal about the local market. Even simple things, such as:

- what size bars are usually sold
- where customers usually buy their chocolate
- whether there are regulations affecting ingredients
- whether the ingredients have to be listed

- what the prices of the competitors' products are
- whether the label should be in another language

might all cause problems for a UK producer who has not completed the necessary market research. Cadbury's is large enough to rely on its international brand name but smaller chocolate producers would need to complete extensive research before selling abroad.

ⒸASE STUDY

Is the market the same?

It would be difficult to tell the difference between the products sold overseas and the same products sold in the UK. Body Shop sells the same items in its overseas markets as it does in the UK. Its strategy is to rely on the worldwide image of its products and not make any changes when selling abroad.

ⒸASE STUDY

The market is different

In some situations there are obvious differences in the home and overseas market. All BMW cars manufactured for sale in the UK have to be right hand drive. This creates the need for a slightly different product. BMW therefore has to incur additional costs in preparing for this particular overseas market.

These case studies show three of the many different approaches to selling overseas:

- Cadbury's sells the same item in Austria as in the UK but the labelling is different
- Body Shop sells exactly the same items overseas as it sells in the UK
- BMW sells in the UK a different product to the cars it sells in Germany.

Deciding which approach to take (or possibly another approach) is one of the reasons why international competitiveness is more difficult to sustain than just competing in the home market. In these examples each business has an international reputation to rely upon, thereby making exporting easier.

ACTIVITY

We are all used to buying imported products. Any visit to a supermarket will illustrate the range of imported products sold in the UK. Select five imported products from a supermarket and analyse how the overseas company is selling to the UK. Some of the things to consider are as follows:

1 Is it sold under the supermarket's own label range?
2 What languages are used on the packaging?
3 Is it identical to the product sold in the home market (can you tell)?
4 Is it cheaper than the UK equivalent?

Compare the results you have observed with similar results from another member of your group. Are there any general observations you can make about the competitiveness of imported food in the UK?

Selling a product in an overseas market is not the same as selling in the UK. If a business is working in a market that it does not fully understand there are many things that can go wrong and hinder success:

- language difficulties
- legislation may vary
- technical requirements may vary
- distribution channels may be different
- the need for greater financial resources, such as insurance and shipping costs
- consumers' tastes may vary
- the level of overseas competition may be unknown
- the exchange rate may change.

Exchange rate

ACTIVITY

British tourists have always enjoyed self-catering holidays in France. The demand for these holidays is influenced by prices in France and more importantly the value of sterling. When the value of the French franc fell in 1997, the cost of a holiday in France fell. Although the price in French francs did not change, the cost for UK tourists had fallen because of the change in the **exchange rate**.

Table 2.13 *Exchange rates effects*

	Cost of holiday in French francs	Exchange rate	Cost of holiday in £
2-week self-catering holiday for 4 people	4800	£1 = 8ff	600
The same 2-week self-catering holiday for 4 people	4800	£1 = 10ff	480

1 What has been the percentage change in price for this holiday for UK visitors?
2 What are the implications for the providers of the self-catering holidays of this change in the exchange rate?

Key term

The **exchange rate** is the value of one country's currency expressed in terms of how much of another country's currency can be bought.

Changes in the value of sterling are outside the control of any company but they can cause considerable problems for business. When sterling has a high value, British goods are expensive abroad and demand from overseas consumers will fall. When sterling has a low value, British goods are less expensive abroad and the demand from overseas consumers will be higher. Even though the price in the UK has not changed, changes in overseas prices affect the total demand for a business's products. For example, if a British company sells a milling machine to Germany for 2 million Deutschmarks when the exchange rate is £1 = DM2.5, then the British company expects to receive £800,000. If the exchange rate changes to £1 = DM3.2 when payment is made, then the British company will receive only £625,000.

Want to know more?

Many organisations try to protect themselves from changes in the exchange rate. Some of the approaches used include:
- suppliers sending invoices in their own currency and requiring buyers to take all the risks involved in currency fluctuations
- arranging, with a bank or other financial institution, to buy foreign currency at an agreed rate on the day the invoice is settled
- adding a clause to the contract to cover exchange rate fluctuations
- buying the foreign currency at the same time as the contract is signed.

Coping with the exchange rate

In the summer of 1997 the value of sterling rose quickly, creating problems for British exporters. Pal International, based in Leicester, is one of the world's leading suppliers of chef's hats to Paris restaurants. All of its sales to France are in the local currency and the rise in the value of sterling reduced income by 30 per cent in one year. To remain competitive, the company was not able to increase its prices in France. To remain profitable, the company had to develop other ways of increasing income or cutting costs. This is the dilemma facing all exporters when sterling rises in value. Pal International's approach was to increase its marketing activities in other parts of the world where the company did not suffer the same problems with the high value of sterling. This policy of diversification, into new regions of the world, allowed Pal to remain competitive despite the rise in the exchange rates.

Source: adapted from *The Observer*, 13 July 1997

National reputations

Countries develop their own reputations which can be used to the advantage of individual businesses. Italy is renowned for its design and style, Germany for its efficiency, Japan for its technical expertise – these reputations help businesses sell in their overseas markets. The UK has expertise in the music industry and the fashion trade. This international reputation helps all businesses in these markets to sell abroad.

Competitive advantage

Figure 2.39 considers the place of a UK business in an international context. The analysis considers the strengths of each business and considers its chances of success in the world market. The diagram shows four different types of business within a world market. Businesses can

		Competitive advantage	
		Lower cost	Differentiation
Competitive scope	Broad target	Cost leadership	Differentiation
	Narrow target	Cost focus	Focused differentiation

Figure 2.39 Competitive advantage

have two types of advantage over their competitors: lower costs or the
ability to differentiate their products. In facing the world market,
businesses can either attempt to compete in all areas or be more
selective in their approach.

Michael Porter looked at different strategies used by the same industry
in different countries to improve performance. The four generic
strategies shown above can be used to explain how some businesses
operate. His analysis argued that all businesses should focus on one of
these four strategies in order to be successful in international markets:

1 offer a wide variety of products at premium prices (differentiation
   strategy)
2 offer lower quality, cheaper products (cost leadership)
3 offer specialist products at premium prices (focused differentiation)
4 offer simple, standardised products at very low cost (cost focus).

The first two strategies are very broad and allow a business to compete
in a large number of areas. The other two strategies focus on a small
number of products or services where the home producer has a chance
of success. Businesses can succeed with any of these four strategies.
Businesses that are stuck in the middle, simultaneously trying to follow
more than one strategy, will not be successful.

Examples of these general strategies can be seen throughout different
industries:

- in the clothing industry, countries specialising in haute couture
  follow strategy 3 while developing countries follow strategy 4
- in the international toy market, countries with low labour costs
  follow strategy 2, whereas the USA has adopted strategy 1 and
  Japan has followed strategy 3 by concentrating on electronic games.

Although this analysis applies to countries and how they should
compete, it affects individual businesses since they are able to follow a
national trend and gain advantage from the general reputation that a
country has in particular product areas.

Helping British competitiveness

There are a number of organisations that provide help to British
businesses. The main government support is from the Department of
Trade and Industry whose emphasis is on developing British
competitiveness (see www.tradepartners.gov.uk for help with exporting).
Other organisations include:

- local Chambers of Commerce
- Trade Associations
- the large clearing banks
- Training and Enterprise Councils
- local enterprise agencies
- European Information Centres designed for small and medium sized
  businesses to take advantage of the Single European Market
- the Business Links network of 'one-stop shops' for business support
- economic development units in local authorities.

 Buy British, page 56

69

Barriers to trade, page 59

Barriers to trade, page 59

Key term

A **multinational** is any organisation that manufactures and trades in more than one country. These businesses are sometimes called transnationals.

ACTIVITY

Investigate what organisations exist in your area of the country to support British businesses who wish to sell abroad. Produce a list of these organisations and explain how each of them can assist an existing business that wishes to expand overseas.

Transnational corporations

Large corporations that manufacture and trade in more than one country have a great deal of power and are often able to find ways around any barriers to trade. These transnational corporations, also known as **multinationals**, are able to move their investments to the most profitable location. For example, many international car producers have their factories in the UK. This allows them to manufacture within the European Union and trade within the EU without any barriers. If the cars were produced in the USA or Japan, there might be restrictions on their export or sale in the EU.

Transnational corporations compete with nationally based companies in many countries. The size and resources of these businesses make it more difficult for small companies to compete effectively. One of the advantages held by small businesses, in these circumstances, is their ability to be flexible and to change to meet the needs of the market. Transnationals are often bureaucratic and unable to respond quickly to market needs. The small business, often in touch with the market, can use its flexibility to survive despite the existence of a dominant competitor. In the 1990s most transnationals tried to copy this small business approach by developing what Charles Handy calls the philosophy of 'being global and local' at the same time. This is achieved by using the following strategies:

- removal, often through redundancy, of layers of managers so that the people who make the decisions are close to their customers and not in an office hundreds of miles away
- empowerment of staff, which allows relatively junior staff to make important decisions where they have more up-to-date knowledge and experience of customers' needs
- using new technology to introduce changes more quickly
- decentralisation where head offices are removed and the work completed in offices near to the transnationals' customers
- outsourcing where parts of the business's operations are undertaken by smaller, independent companies which specialise in tasks such as computing, accounting, maintenance and repairs, cleaning, etc. This allows the transnational to concentrate on its core business activities rather than having to undertake everything itself.

All of these five strategies attempt to reduce the centralised, anonymous nature of large businesses and allow them to better understand their markets. This allows the multinational to be more competitive in each of its markets. The 'being global and local' approach allows the resources, know-how and expertise of a large business to be used to compete with small and medium sized firms in each and every market. These competitive strategies are appropriate for multinational businesses which continually need to check that they are not becoming bureaucratic and out of touch.

With improved communications transnational businesses have to be very careful that their actions in one country do not cause problems in another area of the world. The pressure on transnationals to operate at a high standard in terms of environmental protection, social awareness and responsibility in addition to not exploiting less developed economies creates additional pressures. It is important for large businesses to be seen to 'do the right thing' to prevent consumer resistance and protest.

CASE STUDY

Nestlé

Figure 2.40 *The action of pressure groups*

The pressure group, Baby Milk Action, is part of a global network which campaigns to stop the baby feeding industry from promoting the bottle feeding of babies. In unsafe conditions it is very difficult to sterilise bottles and teats, so artificial feeding very often leads to illnesses and can even cause death. Part of the campaign is against Nestlé, the largest food company in the world with over 8500 brands

Key term

A **less developed country** is one where the average income per head of population falls below a certain level.

Conditions of demand,
page 11

including Nescafe instant coffee. This campaign persuades consumers to switch to another product and the conditions of demand for Nescafe instant coffee therefore change, causing the demand curve to fall and move to the left. This effect could be countered by increased advertising by Nescafe or by a change in the company's policy on promoting bottle feeding.

©ASE STUDY

Shopping online

Adding value is an important aspect of maintaining a competitive edge. All businesses strive to stay ahead of the competition, to satisfy the needs of their customers and to meet the requirements of the financiers. For most large businesses the competition is global and not limited to existing UK based businesses. Many industries have seen continual changes as the forces of competition lead to increased innovation. In food retailing these changes sometimes appear never-ending:

- takeover activity; e.g. Asda is now owned by Wal-Mart, Kwik-save by Somerfield
- low cost competition, e.g. Costcutters
- introduction of organic produce, e.g. Waitrose
- loyalty cards, e.g. Tesco
- 24 hour opening, e.g. Sainsbury.

One of the newest ways to compete is by online shopping. In 2000 Tesco announced plans for the expansion of its current service in 100 stores to 50 per cent of all stores by the end of the year. With online grocery sales in the UK expected to rise from £165 million in 1999 to £2.3 billion in 2004, Tesco cannot risk not offering this service. Online shopping has a number of advantages:

- Tesco can use existing stores rather than building new ones as a way of increasing sales, thereby earning greater income from its existing fixed assets
- online shopping creates loyal customers who are likely to reorder
- information about online customers is readily available and can be used to set marketing strategies
- Tesco is seen as encouraging a reduction in car use with the associated environmental benefits.

Online shopping is still a small percentage of total grocery sales and out-of-town centres are unlikely to disappear. There are significant costs associated with setting up and maintaining a reliable online ordering system but the potential benefits are large.

Tasks

1 Compare Tesco's store prices and online prices.
2 How could Tesco use information from online shoppers to design their marketing policies?
3 Investigate what services other retailers offer online.
4 Are there any disadvantages for Tesco in encouraging online shopping?
5 How do you think other grocery retailers will respond to this expansion in Tesco's services to its customers?

Appendix

Key Legislation

Data Protection Acts (1984, 1998)

These Acts cover businesses, the self-employed and homeworkers who keep information, no matter how little, on computer about any living person. Almost any information other than a name, address and telephone number (with a few other exceptions) places an obligation to register with the Data Protection Registrar. Individuals have the right to see any computerised information held on them and to have incorrect information amended or deleted.

Once a business is registered, a Code of Practice is issued which requires the business to:

- keep the information secure
- ensure the information is accurate and relevant to its needs
- comply with individuals' right to see any computerised information held on them and to have incorrect information amended or deleted.

EU Council Directive (90/270) (1993)

The directive lays down minimum safety and health requirements for the users of computer screens or visual display units (VDU). Employers (including home workers) are expected to evaluate the risk to themselves and their staff from computer equipment, software and the working environment.

Health and Safety at Work Act (1974)
Updated by: Workplace Health and Safety Welfare
Regulations 1992 (EC Directives)

Employers should ensure the provision of adequate toilet and washing facilities, machines that are electrically safe, and protective clothing or equipment; they must ensure that precautions are taken when using chemicals; they must provide and a clean and tidy workplace for their workforce. The self-employed, home workers and people who work alone away from employer's premises are included.

Employers are required to:

- provide systems of work that are, so far as is reasonably practicable, safe and without risk to health.

Employees have a responsibility to:

- take reasonable care of themselves and other people affected by their work
- co-operate with their employers in the discharge of their legal obligations.

Human Rights Act (1998)

This came into effect in October 2000 and covers everything a public authority (local government, national government, government agency, etc) does. It provides a basis for the protection of the fundamental rights of every citizen. All public authorities have an obligation to ensure that respect for human rights is at the core of their day-to-day work. Questions that public authorities need to ask include the following:

- Is a person's ability to carry out a trade or profession adversely affected?
- Is a person's physical or mental well-being adversely affected?
- Is a person's private or family life adversely affected?
- Is any individual or group being discriminated against, on any basis?

If the answer to these types of question is yes, an individual may be able to bring legal action against the public authority.

Social Chapter (1997)

The Maastricht Summit in December 1991 adopted the 'Social Chapter' within the European Union. The UK accepted this in 1997. Some of the main sections of the Social Chapter are:

- freedom of movement within Europe
- the right of all EU nationals to receive equal treatment as nationals of the host nation
- all employment is to be 'fairly remunerated'
- the establishment of controls on the organisation and flexibility of working time, including a maximum working week
- protection for employees engaged in other than full-time jobs of indefinite duration (part-timers, temporary workers, shift-workers, etc)
- the right to annual leave and a weekly rest period
- every EC citizen to have 'adequate social protection'
- the right to a 'minimum income' for all workers excluded from the labour market without being able to claim unemployment benefit
- the right of employees to belong to any professional organisation or trade union
- the freedom to negotiate and conclude collective agreements
- the right to take collective action, e.g. to strike
- equal treatment between men and women
- further developments to ensure satisfactory health and safety conditions at work, including a movement to standardise in the European Union
- a minimum age of employment of 16
- the right of young workers to vocational training for at least two years.

Index